UNION PACIFIC
RAILROAD HERITAGE

A freight train near the Great Overland Station in Topeka, Kansas, on September 1, 2021 is headed by Union Pacific Railroad diesel locomotive No. 7623 built by General Electric Company (GE) in February 2007 (GE designation ES44AC; Union Pacific [UP] designation C45ACCTE with C = six axles; 45 = evolution series locomotive [designed to meet the US EPA's Tier 2 locomotive emissions standards for 2005] because while the locomotive can make 4,500 horsepower, it requires 100 horsepower to run the auxiliary so the available horsepower is 4,400; AC = alternating current; and CTE = unit is equipped with a feature known as Controlled Tractive Effort). By definition, tractive effort is the force exerted by the locomotive to turn its wheels causing them to revolve allowing the locomotive to move along the rails. Between the large United States flag painted on the locomotive and locomotive cab, the locomotive is lettered "Building America." (*Brian A. Keates photograph*)

On a beautiful March 21, 2021, Union Pacific Railroad diesel locomotive No. 2522 (type ES44AC-H built by General Electric Company [GE] in February 2015 with a Chessie Seaboard autorack behind it) is at East Syracuse, New York. (*Brian A. Keates photograph*)

UNION PACIFIC
RAILROAD HERITAGE

Beth Anne Keates and Kenneth C. Springirth

On September 2, 2021, Union Pacific Railroad diesel locomotives No. 3041 (type SD70AH-T4 built by built by Electro Motive Division of General Motors Corporation [EMD] in January 2017) and No. 8066 (type AC45CCTE built by GE in May 2013) are leading a grain train in Topeka, Kansas south across the Kansas River. (*Brian A. Keates photograph*)

On top portion of front cover: The Union Pacific Railroad yard at Topeka, Kansas, is the location of diesel locomotives No. 8897 (type SD70AH built by EMD in 2014) and No. 7611 (GE designation ES44AC; UP designation C45ACCTE built in January 2007). (*Brian A. Keates photograph*)

On bottom portion of front cover: Union Pacific Railroad Big Boy steam locomotive No. 4014 is at a stopover at Topeka, Kansas, in this photograph taken at 6:30 p.m. on August 31, 2021. (*Brian A. Keates photograph*)

Back cover: In a special "Salute to the military tour" paint scheme, Union Pacific Railroad locomotive No. 1943 (originally No. 9026 type SD70AH built by EMD and delivered in August 2016) is rolling north near Woodbury, New Jersey, on June 3, 2018. According to the October 19, 2017 Union Pacific New Release, "UP No. 1943 spotlights Union Pacific's relationship with thousands of veterans who helped build America after defending the United States—a tradition dating back to the company's founding. Created in collaboration with Union Pacific veterans, the locomotive name is connected to a Boeing B-17 Flying Fortress funded by war bond contributions from Union Pacific employees in 1943. The plane was christened *The Spirit of the Union Pacific* and assigned to the 571st Bomber Squadron. The *Spirit of the Union Pacific* was shot down on its fifth mission during a raid on enemy installations in Münster, Germany." (*Brian A. Keates* photograph).

America Through Time is an imprint of Fonthill Media LLC
www.through-time.com | office@through-time.com

First published 2021

Typeset in Mrs Eaves XL Serif Narrow
Printed and bound in England

Published by Arcadia Publishing by arrangement with Fonthill Media LLC
For all general information, please contact Arcadia Publishing:

Telephone: 843-853-2070
Fax: 843-853-0044
E-mail: sales@arcadiapublishing.com
For customer service and orders:
Toll-Free 1-888-313-2665

www.arcadiapublishing.com

Contents

Acknowledgments

Thanks to the Erie County (Pennsylvania) Public Library system for their inter-library loan system. Pictures of the Gallitzin, Pennsylvania, tunnel area in this book were taken by Bob Elder (Innkeeper of the Tunnel Inn). John Bryan, Dylan Chastain, Brian A. Keates, Beth Anne Keates, Andrew L. Keates, Jacob A. Keates, D. J. Miller, Kenneth C. Springirth and Virginia M. Springirth provided photographs. A number of pictures came from postcards and were (*Used with permission from Audio-Visual Designs [www.audiovisualdesigns.com]*). The names of the photographers who took the pictures for those postcards are as follows: John C. Benson, Henry W. Brueckman, Leo Caloia, Bob Collins, Ken Crist, Frank Ferguson, Ed Fulcomer, George Hamlin, James L. Jeffery, John A. Kirchner, Richard G. Nash, Mac Owen, S. D. Rippeteau, John T. Roderick, Louis L. Stein Jr., R. R. Wallin, William I. White Jr., and Douglas C. Worman. Jerry and Lynda Anderson contributed to the history of the Overland Station.

The *North Platte Telegraph* newspaper, Union Pacific website www.up.com, and Form 10-K Reports were important information sources. Books that served as excellent reference sources were: *June 1916 Official Guide of the Railways*, *Norfolk Southern Locomotive Directory 2017–2018* by Paul K. Withers, *The Big Legacy of the Union Pacific Big Boy* by James J. Reisdorff and Michael M. Bartels, *The First Transcontinental Railroad* by John Debo Galloway, *Union Pacific's Big Boys* by editor Jeff Wilson and book design by Lisa Bergman, *Union Pacific Locomotive Directory 1998* by Don Strack, *Union Pacific Locomotive Directory 2005–2007* by Paul K. Withers, *Union Pacific Locomotive Directory 2007–2012* by Paul K. Withers, and *Westward to Promontory* by Barry B. Combs.

This book is dedicated to Donald P. van Krieken Sr., the father of co-author Beth Anne Keates, who encouraged his daughter to become knowledgeable about our rail heritage and its importance to the development of the United States.

Union Pacific Railroad 4,400-horsepower diesel electric locomotive No. 5621 with AC traction motors (GE designation AC4400CW; UP designation C44ACCTE placed in service on October 13, 2004) with a Ferromex (Ferrocarril Mexicano or Mexican Railway which is a private rail system [Union Pacific Railroad owns 26 percent of the company] operating 5,970 miles of track in Mexico and connects with five cities on the United States border) locomotive behind it are pulling a general manifest freight train eastbound through Topeka, Kansas, on September 1, 2021. (*Brian A. Keates photograph*)

Introduction

During the 1849 United States Gold Rush, thousands of people arrived in California. To reach California, they had a choice by sea (either via Cape Horn or by the dangerous fever area through Panama) or by land (facing possible Indian attack, huge waterless areas, and incredible physical exertion). By 1860, California's population had reached 300,000. Congress was unable to act even though there was increasing public support for building a railroad to the Pacific. Fort Sumter was fired upon on April 12, 1861, and three weeks later eleven southern states broke away from the United States which was engulfed in a Civil War. With no opposition to a northern route, the Pacific Railroad Act was approved by Congress and signed into law by President Abraham Lincoln on July 1, 1862 to incorporate the Union Pacific Railroad to construct the railroad from the Missouri River to the Pacific Ocean. Private investment was encouraged by providing the railroad with a grant of government lands and a loan of government bonds. In addition, an Act of Congress established that the track would be 4 feet 8.5 inches standard gauge. Construction, by thousands of immigrants, was to go westward from Council Bluffs, Iowa, to meet the Central Pacific line. The combined Union Pacific–Central Pacific line became known as the First Transcontinental Railroad and later the Overland Route. In *Westward to Promontory* by Barry B. Combs, it was noted: "Only about one in four were tracklayers. The immigrants were graders, teamsters, herdsmen, cooks, bakers, blacksmiths, bridge builders, carpenters, masons, and clerks. On the average they made three dollars a day, good wages for the times." The Central Pacific Railroad was chartered by the U.S. Congress in 1862 to build a railroad from Sacramento, California, east to complete the western part of the First Transcontinental Railroad in the United States. Construction began in 1865, and by 1868, there were 12,000 Chinese laborers representing most of the work force. On April 28, 1869, Central Pacific Railroad track workers set a record of laying 10 miles of track. Facing mountains and severe weather, the two lines came together at Promontory Summit, Utah, 53 miles west of Ogden, Utah, on May 10, 1869 where the Golden Spike was driven. The Central Pacific Railroad completed 742 miles of track from Sacramento, California, to Ogden, Utah, and the Union Pacific Railroad completed 1,032 miles of track from Omaha, Nebraska, to Ogden, Utah. In 1885, the Central Pacific Railroad was acquired by the Southern Pacific Company.

Groundbreaking for the Utah Central Railroad, formed to connect Salt Lake City to the transcontinental railroad at Ogden, was on May 17, 1869 at Ogden, and the line was completed on January 10, 1870 with passenger service beginning on January 12, 1870. The Utah Southern Railway was built in stages with construction beginning at Salt Lake City on May 2, 1871 and dates of first operation as follows: August 9, 1872 to Draper; September 27, 1872 to Lehi; September 23, 1873 to American Fork; November 25, 1873 to Provo; February 2, 1875 to York; and June 13, 1879 to Juab. Connecting with the Union Pacific Railroad portion of the transcontinental railroad, the 3-foot narrow gauge Utah Northern Railway began grading during the first week of September 1871 four miles south of Brigham City and completed the line to Butte, Montana, on December 15, 1881. Union Pacific gained control of the Utah Southern in June 1875 and the Utah Central in 1878. The Union Pacific Railroad acquired the Utah Northern Railway in April 1878, reorganized it as the Utah & Northern Railway, and completed the line to Butte, Montana, on December 31, 1881. On July 25, 1887, the Utah & Northern Railway was converted to standard gauge. On January 24, 1880, the original Union Pacific Railroad was purchased by stockholder Jay Gould (owner of the Kansas Pacific), and the original Union Pacific Rail Road became "Union Pacific Railway." During the Panic of 1893 (an economic depression in the United States that began in 1893 and ended in 1897 and effected every sector of the economy), the Union Pacific Railway declared bankruptcy on October 13, 1893. Large construction expenditures, dramatic decline in revenue, and growing debt contributed to that bankruptcy. A new Union Pacific "Railroad" was formed, and Union Pacific Railway was merged into that corporation.

On March 8, 1904, the 102-mile Lucin Cutoff opened between Ogden and Lucin. It had a 12-mile trestle crossing the Great Salt Lake that was in use from 1904 to the late 1950s when it was replaced by a dirt and rock causeway. This cutoff bypassed Promontory Summit cutting 44 miles off the original route. Noting that farmers in Central and Salinas Valleys of California grew more produce than could be locally sold, on December 7, 1906, the Union Pacific Railroad and Southern Pacific Company formed Pacific Fruit Express that began operation on October 1, 1907 with a fleet of 6,600 refrigerator cars built by American Car & Foundry Company.

The original Western Pacific Railroad, established in 1862, built the westernmost part of the First Transcontinental Railroad between Sacramento and Oakland, California, and was absorbed into the Central Pacific Railroad in 1870. A new Western Pacific Railway acquired the Alameda and San Joaquin Railroad and completed the Feather River Route in 1909. The Union Pacific Railroad purchased the Western Pacific Railroad on December 22, 1982.

The Chicago & Eastern Illinois Railroad (C&EI), organized in 1877, was a consolidation of three railroads: Chicago, Danville &

Vincennes Railroad; Evansville, Terre Haute & Chicago Railroad; and the Evansville & Terre Haute Railroad. During the Great Depression, the C&EI went bankrupt in 1933, reemerged from bankruptcy in 1940, and was merged into the Missouri Pacific Railroad in October 15, 1976.

The Texas & Pacific Railway was created by federal charter in 1871 to build a southern transcontinental railroad between Marshall, Texas, and San Diego, California. While it never reached San Diego, it connected with the Southern Pacific at Sierra Blanca, Texas, in 1881. Missouri Pacific Railroad gained majority ownership of Texas & Pacific Railway's stock in 1928; however, they allowed it to continue operating as a separate entity until the merger occurred on October 15, 1976.

The Midland Valley Railroad (named for Midland, Arkansas, a coal mining town in western Arkansas which was served by the railroad) was incorporated on June 4, 1903 to build a line from Hope, Arkansas, via Tulsa, Oklahoma, to Wichita, Kansas. Owned by the Muskogee Company, the Midland Valley Railroad acquired the Kansas, Oklahoma & Gulf Railroad in 1925, and the Muskogee Company purchased the Oklahoma City–Ada–Atoka Railway in 1929. The Muskogee Company authorized the sale of all three railroad stocks to the Texas & Pacific Railway in 1962. Texas & Pacific Railway sold Oklahoma City–Ada–Atoka Railway to the Atchison Topeka & Santa Fe Railway with which it merged on December 1, 1967. Midland Valley Railroad merged into Texas & Pacific Railway on April 1, 1967. Kansas, Oklahoma & Gulf Railroad merged into Texas & Pacific Railway on April 1, 1970.

Ground was broken for the Pacific Railroad in St. Louis on July 4, 1851. After a railroad debt crisis, the Pacific Railroad was reorganized as the Missouri Pacific Railroad in 1872. Missouri Pacific Railroad declared bankruptcy in 1933. It entered into trusteeship, reorganized, and the trusteeship ended in 1956. Under Downing B. Jenks, who became president and chief executive in 1961, Missouri Pacific Railroad became a pioneer in the early years of computer-guided rail technology. It was a major hauler of coal, grain, ore, automobiles, dry goods, and shipping containers. On December 22, 1982, the Missouri Pacific Railroad was purchased by the Union Pacific Corporation and combined with the Western Pacific Railroad and Union Pacific Railroad to form Pacific Rail Systems; however, all three railroads maintained their own identity. On January 1, 1997, the Missouri Pacific Railroad officially merged into the Union Pacific Railroad.

The Missouri, Kansas and Texas Railway was incorporated in May 1870 and received government land grants to build a railroad connecting frontier military posts of Fort Riley, Fort Gibson, and Fort Scott. With KT its abbreviation in timetables and stock exchange symbol, the railroad in the 1890s was informally referred to as "Katy." On June 6, 1870, Missouri, Kansas and Texas Railroad rails reached Kansas, and construction continued southward reaching Texas in 1872. Acquiring other small railroads, Missouri, Kansas and Texas Railroad reached Dallas in 1886, Waco in 1888, Houston in 1893, and San Antonio in 1901. A major asset for the Missouri, Kansas and Texas Railway was its short route from

Kansas City, Kansas, to San Antonio plus a line to Galveston, Texas. Missouri, Kansas and Texas Railroad was purchased by Union Pacific Railroad through its subsidiary Missouri Pacific Railroad on August 12, 1988 and became part of the Union Pacific Railroad on December 1, 1989.

The Tomah & Lake St. Croix Railroad was organized on April 1, 1863, taken over in 1866 by the West Wisconsin Railway, and following expansions and consolidations was purchased by the Chicago, St. Paul, & Minneapolis Railway which after a 1880 merger with the North Wisconsin Railway became the Chicago, St. Paul, Minneapolis & Omaha Railroad. In 1882, the majority of its stock was purchased by the Chicago & North Western. Its official identity was maintained until 1972.

The Minneapolis & St. Louis Railway was created on May 26, 1870 to establish a railroad connection between Minneapolis and south agricultural regions. Some of the largest flour milling operations in the United States were located in Minneapolis. Wheat was the main item grown in southern Minnesota and northern Iowa. Land was sold to prospective farmers at favorable rates with the railroad hoping to make profits by shipping farm products out and home goods in, and small towns were established as shipping points and commercial centers with the goal of attracting more businessmen and farmers. The Minneapolis & St. Louis Railway was able to remain independent even though it was in serious financial trouble. In 1935, Lucian Sprague took over as receiver (one appointed by a court to administer a property in bankruptcy), significant abandonments were made, and receivership ended in 1943. On November 1, 1960, Chicago & North Western acquired the Minneapolis & St. Louis Railway.

The Litchfield & Madison Railway, incorporated on March 1, 1900, took over an isolated line of the Chicago, Peoria & St. Louis Railroad between Litchfield and Madison (both in Illinois), and in 1926 constructed a connection to the Chicago & North Western at Benld, Illinois. On January 2, 1958, the Litchfield & Madison Railway was merged into the Chicago & North Western.

The Minnesota & North Western in 1884 began constructing a railroad south from St. Paul, Minnesota to Dubuque, Iowa. In 1892, the railroad reorganized as the Chicago Great Western which by acquiring other railroad lines established routes west to Omaha, Nebraska; south to St. Joseph, Missouri; and east to Chicago, Illinois. It merged into the Chicago & North Western Railway on July 1, 1968.

The Chicago & Rock Island Railroad began construction on October 1, 1851, and its first train operated on October 10, 1852 between Chicago and Joliet (both in Illinois). The Chicago & Rock Island Railroad acquired the Mississippi & Missouri Railroad on July 6, 1866 and formed the Chicago, Rock Island & Pacific Railroad Company (Rock Island). Through construction and acquisitions, the Rock Island to the east reached Chicago and Memphis, to the west reached Denver, to the south reached Galveston, and to the north reached Minneapolis. Following an August 1979 labor strike, the railroad shut down. John W. Ingram became president and CEO of the Rock Island, and the system gradually resumed operation in a very efficient manner. However, because of the precarious financial condition of the Rock Island, the Interstate Commerce Commission declared a transportation emergency and rejected its reorganization plan. The final train arrived during a massive snow storm in Denver on March 31, 1980. The following railroads acquired large portions of the Rock Island: Cotton Belt 965 miles, Chicago & North Western 750 miles, and a subsidiary of the Katy 645 miles. These railroads were later merged into the Union Pacific.

In 1855, the Chicago, St. Paul & Fond du Lac Railroad was started to go northwest from near Chicago, and was reorganized in 1859 by the Chicago & North Western Railway. On February 15, 1865, it merged with the Galena & Chicago Union Railroad. Chicago & Northwestern Railroad was the first railroad to connect with the UP at Council Bluffs in 1867. Employees of Chicago & Northwestern Railroad purchased the railroad in 1968, and it was renamed Chicago & Northwestern Transportation Company. In May 1994, the Chicago & Northwestern Transportation Company reverted to its original name Chicago & North Western Railway whose stock was acquired by the Union Pacific Railroad on April 27, 1995. On June 23, 1995, Chicago & North Western Railway was merged into Union Pacific Railroad.

The St. Louis Southwestern Railway, known as Cotton Belt, was organized on January 15, 1891 and gained trackage rights over the Missouri Pacific Railroad on October 18, 1903 along the eastern shore of the Mississippi River to reach East St. Louis, Illinois, where it used Terminal Railroad Association trackage rights into East St. Louis. Southern Pacific Company took control of the St. Louis Southwestern Railway on April 14, 1932.

The Northwestern Pacific Railroad (which has played a major role in the growth of Northern California) was created in 1907 through the consolidation of six separate companies held by the Atchison, Topeka & Santa Fe Railroad and Southern Pacific Railroad. In 1929, the Southern Pacific Railroad purchased the Atchison, Topeka & Santa Fe Railroad interest in the line, and the Northwestern Pacific Railroad has been a wholly-owned subsidiary of the Southern Pacific Railroad. In 1984, trackage from Willits to Eureka was sold to a new company, the Eureka Southern Railroad later named North Coast Railroad. The line came under control of the Golden Gate Bridge, Highway & Transportation District plus Marin and Sonoma Counties, and a new operator NWP Company, Inc. was selected under a bidding process to operate the line in May 2006. The line was reopened in June 2011 and began operating over a section of track between Lombard and Windsor, California.

The Southern Pacific Railroad was founded in 1865 to build a railroad line from San Francisco to San Diego. On February 17, 1885, the Southern Pacific and Central Pacific combined under a holding company named the Southern Pacific Company. In 1969, the Southern Pacific Transportation Company absorbed the Southern Pacific Company which merged with the Union Pacific Railroad on September 11, 1996.

The original Denver & Rio Grande Western Railway built a narrow-gauge line from Ogden, Utah, to Grand Junction, Colorado, which became the Rio Grande Western Railway in 1889 as part of a plan to upgrade the line from narrow to standard gauge. In 1934, the Dotsero Cutoff was completed giving Denver a direct transcontinental link to the west. On September 12, 1988, Rio Grande Industries (which controlled the Denver & Rio Grande Western Railway) purchased the Southern Pacific and combined the systems on October 13, 1988 under the name Southern Pacific. On September 11, 1996, Union Pacific and Southern Pacific merged.

The Denver, Northwestern & Pacific Railway (DNW&P) began construction in 1902. DNW&P tracks climbed Rollins Pass with a series of switchback loops with a steep 4 percent grade. Severe snow conditions on the original line made it unprofitable to operate. David Moffat of the DNW&P laid out a route for a tunnel that would cut through the Continental Divide; however, he was unable to raise the funds to build that tunnel before he died in 1911. The DNW&P was reorganized as the Denver & Salt Lake Railway (D&SL) in July 1912. On April 29, 1922 the Moffat Tunnel Improvement District was created, and the railroad tunnel was holed through on July 7, 1927. The Moffat Tunnel was opened on February 26, 1928. With the completion of the Dotsero Cutoff from Dotsero (east of Glenwood Springs) to connect with the D&SL at Bond on the Colorado River in 1934, railroad connections through the Moffat Tunnel shortened the distance between Denver and the Pacific coast by 176 miles. Denver & Salt Lake Railway was merged into the Denver & Rio Grande Western on April 11, 1947.

The Sacramento Northern Railway was formed by taking over the Northern Electric Railway operating from Sacramento north to Maysville-Yuba and Chico (all in California) in 1918 plus the San Francisco–Sacramento Railroad operating from Sacrament south to Oakland in 1928. Western Pacific Railroad purchased the Sacramento Northern Railway in 1922 which no longer existed after the Union Pacific Railroad purchased the Western Pacific Railroad on December 22, 1982.

The Spokane International Railway was built by businessman Daniel Chas Corbin with an agreement between Corbin and the Canadian Pacific Railway that the Canadian Pacific Railway would fund much of the line's construction plus secure the loan by holding the Spokane International Railway's bonds. Completion of the Spokane International Railway meant that the Canadian Pacific Railway could compete with the Northern Pacific Railway and Great Northern Railway lines for transportation between the Midwest and the Puget Sound area. Following financial difficulties, the line was reorganized on October 1, 1941 as the Spokane International Railroad and was formally merged into the Union Pacific Railroad on December 31, 1987.

Over its 160 years, the Union Pacific Railroad helped to bring in people to settle the west. During World Wars I and II, the Union Pacific Railroad moved supplies and personnel. In addition during World War II, the railroad maintained servicemen's canteens and United Service Organizations (USO) at stops such as Omaha, North Platte, Pocatello, and Boise.

In this 1966 postcard, American Locomotive Company (Alco) had introduced 1,500-horsepower center cab type Century 415 diesel electric switcher locomotive for improved visibility in both directions which became Chicago, Rock Island & Pacific Railroad (Rock Island) locomotive No. 420 built in September 1966. Ten of these locomotives (Nos. 415–424) were built for the Rock Island. (*Alco Locomotive, Inc. Used with permission from Audio-Visual Designs [www.audiovisualdesigns.com]*)

Rock Island diesel electric 2,000-horsepower EMD type E7 passenger train diesel electric locomotive No. 538 is at the city of Rock Island, Illinois, station powering a westbound passenger train in this May 14, 1950 postcard. (*Photographer Bob Collins Used with permission from Audio-Visual Designs [www.audiovisualdesigns.com]*)

In this December 1, 1966 postcard, Rock Island 2,000-horsepower No. 621 type DL-109 (DL stands for diesel locomotive) built by Alco in October 1941 is at Memphis, Tennessee, waiting to get back to Little Rock, and points west with train No. 21. (*Photographer William I. White Jr. Used with permission from Audio-Visual Designs [www.audiovisualdesigns.com]*)

In this September 10, 1972 postcard, Rock Island 2,000-horsepower diesel electric locomotive No. 630 (EMD type E6A built in October 1941) in a special gold paint scheme on the nose of the locomotive celebrating the fiftieth anniversary of EMD, is shown on a special excursion in Chicago, Illinois. (*Photographer R.R. Wallin Used with permission from Audio-Visual Designs [www. audiovisualdesigns.com]*)

From left to right: steam locomotive No. 4501 (a 2-8-2 wheel arrangement Ms-class Mikado built in October 1911 by Baldwin Locomotive Works for the Southern Railway and was purchased in 1964 by Paul H. Merriman and later given to the Tennessee Valley Railroad Museum) poses with Rock Island type E6 diesel locomotive No. 630 outside the LaSalle Street Station in Chicago on June 24, 1973. This was a special "Green & Gold Rocket" steam excursion special over the Rock Island to Bureau, Illinois, sponsored by the R.R. Club of Chicago. (*Photographer S.D. Rippeteau Used with permission from Audio-Visual Designs [www.audiovisualdesigns.com]*)

A Chicago, Rock Island & Pacific Railroad three car "Rocky Mountain Rocket" powered by 2,000-horsepower diesel electric type E7A locomotive No. 635 (built in 1946) is at the Denver Terminal for an eastbound trip to Omaha and Chicago in this May 1966 postcard. This train was once a deluxe coach and Pullman streamliner. Shortly after this picture was taken, the Rocket was discontinued. (*Photographer K.C. Crist Used with permission from Audio-Visual Designs [www.audiovisualdesigns.com]*)

Three Rock Island locomotives headed by 2,250-horsepower EMD type E8A diesel electric passenger locomotive No. 655, built in March 1952 with some upfront deadhead extra cars from a football special are on the Quad Cities Rocket at the city of Joliet in Will and Kendall Counties, Illinois, in this November 14, 1971 postcard scene. (*Photographer George Hamlin Used with permission from Audio-Visual Designs [www.audiovisualdesigns.com]*)

In this June 1970 postcard, Rock Island diesel electric locomotive No. 751 is in Chicago push pull commuter service in a deep crimson with yellow front paint scheme. This was one of two custom-built 1,000-horsepower type AB6 booster car bodies (Nos. 750 and 751), built in June 1940 by Electro Motive Corporation (EMC), that were built for the "Rocky Mountain Rocket" passenger train from Chicago, Illinois, to Limon, Colorado, after which they were divided. One section went to Colorado Springs and the other to Denver, Colorado. In 1965, both units were assigned to Chicago push pull commuter service. Both Nos. 750 and 751 were scrapped in 1974. (*Photographer Ken Crist Used with permission from Audio-Visual Designs [www.audiovisualdesigns.com]*)

Two EMD four-axle 2,000-horsepower type GP38-2 diesel electric locomotives (in a blue and white paint scheme headed by No. 4334 [built in November 1976] named for the "Iowa Falls Gateway Shippers Association" followed by a red GE U-Boat locomotive) are leading a train of coal hopper cars and piggy back freight cars in Des Moines, Iowa, in this December 17, 1976 postcard. (*Photographer James L. Jeffery Used with permission from Audio-Visual Designs [www.audiovisualdesigns.com]*)

In this postcard, Chicago & North Western Railway 2,400-horsepower Alco type RS-27 diesel electric locomotive No. 900, built in March 1962, poses for an official portrait. Only twenty-seven of these locomotives were built. (*Chicago & Northwestern Railway photograph Used with permission from Audio-Visual Designs [www.audiovisualdesigns.com]*)

In this November 1981 postcard, Chicago & North Western Railway EMD type F7A 1,500-horsepower diesel electric locomotives No. 421 (built as No. 4075A in October 1949) and No. 419 (built as No. 4087A in December 1949) are ready to power the Union Pacific/Chicago & North Western Railway Director's special coming from the Wyoming coal fields to Wisconsin Energy's coal-fired Pleasant Prairie power plant in Kenosha County, Wisconsin, which closed on April 10, 2018. (*Photographer John C. Benson Used with permission from Audio-Visual Designs [www.audiovisualdesigns.com]*)

In this late 1960s postcard, the Western Pacific Railroad California Zephyr (eastbound via Salt Lake City and Denver for Chicago) powered by 1,500-horsepower EMD type F7A diesel electric locomotive No. 804A (originally No. 915A built in January 1950) is traveling down the middle of Third Street in Oakland, California. On the right is Western Pacific's Third & Washington Street Station that opened in 1910. In March 1970, the Zephyr made its last run on the Western Pacific. (*Photographer Louis L. Stein, Jr. Used with permission from Audio-Visual Designs [www.audiovisualdesigns.com]*)

Western Pacific Railroad eastbound California Zephyr headed by 1,500-horsepower EMD type FP7 dual service passenger and freight-hauling diesel locomotive No. 805A (built in January 1950) is in the city of Marysville in Yuba County, California, under the wires of the electrified Sacramento Northern Railway in this April 1965 postcard. The FP7 was basically an EMD F7A locomotive extended by four feet to provide more water capacity for the steam generator for heating passenger trains. (*Photographer John A, Kirchner Used with permission from Audio-Visual Designs [www.audiovisualdesigns.com]*)

In this July 23, 1978 postcard, Western Pacific Railroad EMD type F7A locomotive No. 913, built in January 1950, is shown in the city of Stockton, Joaquin County, California. (*Photographer John C. Benson Used with permission from Audio-Visual Designs [www. audiovisualdesigns.com]*)

Western Pacific Railroad 3,000-horsepower General Electric (GE) type U30B diesel electric locomotive No. 3063, built in May 1969, is leading a train over one leg of the Keddie Wye Bridge in Keddie, California, in this August 1974 postcard scene. This is a railroad junction in the form of a wye that was completed in 1931 on the Western Pacific Railroad (now part of the Union Pacific Railroad) in Plumas County, California. (*Photographer Henry W. Brueckman Used with permission from Audio-Visual Designs [www.audiovisualdesigns.com]*)

In this May 1971 postcard, GE type U30B Western Pacific Railroad diesel electric locomotive No. 771, built in June 1966, is waiting for its next assignment. (*Photographer Henry W. Brueckman Used with permission from Audio-Visual Designs [www.audiovisualdesigns.com]*)

St. Louis Southwestern Railway, known as Cotton Belt, Alco 2,400-horsepower diesel electric locomotive No. 850 type DL-600B is in Memphis, Tennessee, across the Mississippi River from Brinkley, Arkansas, in this December 6, 1965 postcard scene. (*Photographer William I. White Jr. Used with permission from Audio-Visual Designs [www.audiovisualdesigns.com]*)

In this May 7, 1975 postcard, St. Louis Southwestern Railway (known as the Cotton Belt) No. 9389 (six-axle 3,600-horsepower EMD type SD45T-2 diesel electric locomotive built in April 1975 and painted in a Bicentennial color scheme) is at the city of Blue Island in Cook County, Illinois. (*Mac Owen collection Used with permission from Audio-Visual Designs [www.audiovisualdesigns.com]*)

Missouri, Kansas and Texas Railway (informally referred to as Katy) four-axle 3,000-horsepower EMD type GP40 diesel electric locomotive No. 200, built in August 1968, is fresh out of the Parsons, Kansas, shops featuring a new Bicentennial paint scheme with a huge United States flag in this October 1975 postcard scene. (*Photographer Mac Owen Used with permission from Audio-Visual Designs [www.audiovisualdesigns.com]*)

Four EMD type GP39-2 (four-axle 2,300-horsepower) diesel locomotives headed by No. 367, built in April 1984, are powering a merchandise freight train on the Missouri–Kansas–Texas Railroad in this April 4, 1988 postcard. (*Photographer Frank Ferguson Used with permission from Audio-Visual Designs [www.audiovisualdesigns.com]*)

In this postcard scene, Southern Pacific Railroad six-axle 1,000-horsepower Alco type RSD locomotive No. 2876 is powering a train near the city of Kemah in Galveston County, Texas. (*Photographer Mac Owen Used with permission from Audio-Visual Designs [www.audiovisualdesigns.com]*)

A Southern Pacific Railroad passenger train is on the Great Salt Lake Cut Off that extends 102.9 miles from Ogden to Lucin over the north end of the Great Salt Lake in this post card scene. This saved the Southern Pacific Railroad 43.8 miles of distance at a cost of $4.5 million. The 1.5-year project was finished on November 13, 1903. (*Kenneth C. Springirth collection*)

Southern Pacific 1,200-horsepower diesel electric switchers Nos. 2146 and 2148 (type S12 built in 1953 by Baldwin-Lima-Hamilton Corporation) are passing the Santa Fe tower in Los Angeles in this postcard view. (*Photographer Richard G. Nash Used with permission from Audio-Visual Designs [www.audiovisualdesigns.com]*)

In this 1947 postcard view, Southern Pacific steam locomotive No. 4447 with a 4-8-4 wheel arrangement, built by Lima Locomotive Works in 1941, is backing down to the Los Angeles Union Station to couple up to its train in 1947. (*Leo Caloia Collection Used with permission from Audio-Visual Designs [www.audiovisualdesigns.com]*)

In this March 1967 postcard, Southern Pacific diesel electric switcher No. 1000, type SW1 built by EMD in January 1939, is on the Northwestern Pacific between Sausalito and Tiburon, California, in Martin County, California. The name SW1 was based on the locomotive's power (S for 600 horsepower) and frame design (W for welded), and the number 1 distinguished the new design from the previous EMD SW. (*Photographer John A. Kirchner Used with permission from Audio-Visual Designs [www.audiovisualdesigns.com]*)

Steam locomotive No. 4460 with a 4-8-4 wheel arrangement, built by Lima in July 1943, was making Southern Pacific's last steam run as it emerged from the tunnel at Newcastle, California, in this November 1958 postcard. (*Photographer Mac Owen Used with permission from Audio-Visual Designs [www.audiovisualdesigns.com]*)

The Southern Pacific Railroad "Sunset Limited" is making a station stop at San Antonio, Texas, on its westbound trip between New Orleans and Los Angeles in this April 1955 postcard view. The rear sleeping car with its attractive sign was built in 1950. This was an all-weather, year-round route that did not face the massive snows of the Sierra mountain ranges to reach the west coast. (*Photographer Douglas Wornom Used with permission from Audio-Visual Designs [www.audiovisualdesigns.com]*)

Southern Pacific's train No. 76, the "Lark" is southbound at the city of Glendale in Los Angeles County, California, at 8:00 a.m. in this April 16, 1965 postcard scene. This deluxe streamlined sleeping car train between San Francisco's Third and Townsend Station and Los Angeles's Union Station was discontinued on April 8, 1968. (*Photographer Leo Caloia Used with permission from Audio-Visual Designs [www.audiovisualdesigns.com]*)

The open-top observation car used on the Denver & Rio Grande Western Railway provided passengers with an unrestricted view of the marvelous region served by the train in this postcard scene. (*Kenneth C. Springirth collection*)

Denver & Rio Grande Western Railway steam locomotive No. 1801, built in 1937, with a 4-8-4 wheel arrangement is being serviced at the city of Salida in Chafee County, Colorado, where the standard and narrow gauge lines meet in this May 19, 1950 postcard view. (*Photographer Bob Collins Used with permission from Audio-Visual Designs [www.audiovisualdesigns.com]*)

Denver & Rio Grande Western Railway (D&RGW) 4,000-horsepower diesel hydraulic locomotives led by No. 4003 (type ML4000 built by Krauss-Maffei of Munich, Germany and received by D&RGW in November 1961) are east of the city of Helper in Carbon County, Utah, on their July 1962 initial run across the desert. The three units Nos. 4001, 4002, and 4003 were modified to avoid exhaust gases in tunnels; sold to Southern Pacific (SP) on February 6, 1964; were retired by SP on December 31, 1967; and were sold for scrap. (*Photographer Mac Owen Used with permission from Audio-Visual Designs [www.audiovisualdesigns.com]*)

Two Denver & Rio Grande Western Railway diesel units headed by EMD 1,350-horsepower type FT (F stood for 1400 horsepower rounded from 1,350 horsepower and T for twin as it came standard in a two unit set) No. 5484 have arrived at Denver station with the "Royal Gorge" passenger train in this January 1963 postcard scene. This locomotive was built in March 1944 and was retired on March 10, 1964. (*Photographer Ken Crist Used with permission from Audio-Visual Designs [www.audiovisualdesigns.com]*)

In this postcard view, Denver & Rio Grande Western Railway 1,750-horsepower diesel electric locomotive No. 5771 (EMD type F9A built in September 1955) is at the head end of the "Zephyr" passenger train between Denver to Salt Lake City making a station stop at Helper, Utah. This locomotive was retired on September 9, 1996 and was donated to the Colorado Railroad Museum at Golden Colorado and delivered in January 1998. (*Photographer John C. Benson Used with permission from Audio-Visual Designs [www.audiovisualdesigns.com]*)

On a snowy day in March 1962, Denver & Rio Grande Western Railway Alco 2,000-horsepower passenger diesel electric locomotive No. 6013 (Alco type PA1 built as No. 601C in April 1947 and renumbered 6013 on March 6, 1950) has arrived at Winter Park in Grand County, Colorado, with the "Yampa Valley Mail" through a vigorous winter snow storm. (*Photographer Ken Crist Used with permission from Audio-Visual Designs [www.audiovisualdesigns.com]*)

Denver & Rio Grande Western Railway (D&RGW) No. 6013 Alco diesel unit is at the head end of the *Yampa Valley Mail* at Denver, Colorado, in this postcard view. This train connected Denver with the northwestern Colorado town of Craig. The *December 1916 Official Guide of the Railways* shows the 231.4-mile trip from Denver to Craig with thirty scheduled stops required 7.25 hours in each direction. When the United States Post Office ended its D&RGW mail contract in 1963, the train became the *Yampa Valley* which was discontinued on April 7, 1968. (*Mac Owen collection Used with permission from Audio-Visual Designs [www.audiovisualdesigns.com]*)

The Denver & Rio Grande Western Railway eastbound "Royal Gorge" passenger train, powered by locomotive No. 6013, is at Canyon City, Colorado, on a daylight schedule from Salida to Denver through the Royal Gorge in this June 17, 1967 postcard view. This locomotive has a yellow and silver with one black stripe paint scheme compared to the same locomotive in 1962 with yellow and silver with four black stripes shown on page 26. On July 20, 1967, the locomotive was sold to Precision Engineering Company where it was scrapped. (*Photographer Ed Fulcomer Used with permission from Audio-Visual Designs [www.audiovisualdesigns.com]*)

In this December 1965 postcard view, Denver & Rio Grande Western Railway locomotive No. 5764 (EMD type F7A built in July 1952) is leading the streamlined beautiful stainless steel "California Zephyr" passenger train east to Chicago on the "Moffat Tunnel Route" near Cisco in Grand County, Utah (a community that declined with the demise of steam locomotives plus the building of Interstate 70). (*Photographer Ken Crist Used with permission from Audio-Visual Designs [www.audiovisualdesigns.com]*)

Denver & Rio Grande Western Railway type F7 EMD diesel locomotive No. 5571 is on the wye at the East Portal to the Moffat Tunnel in this May 1968 postcard view. (*Photographer John T. Roderick Used with permission from Audio-Visual Designs [www.audiovisualdesigns.com]*)

1

Union Pacific Railroad

As of June 20, 2022, the Union Pacific Railroad is the last United States Class 1 railroad left in the country that has not originated as a merger between separate railroad names or holding companies which makes it the oldest operating Class 1 United States railroad. The original Union Pacific Railroad, founded in 1862, was involved with the First Transcontinental Railroad project that took 12,000 laborers working twelve to sixteen long hours daily seven days a week for six years to connect the United States by rail. Over the last 100 years, the UP acquired the Missouri Pacific Railroad; Chicago & North Western Corporation; Western Pacific Railroad, Missouri–Kansas–Texas Railroad, and Chicago, Rock Island & Pacific Railroad. On September 11, 1996, the Union Pacific Railroad merged with the Southern Pacific Transportation Company using the Southern Pacific name; however, it later reverted back to the Union Pacific Railroad name. Union Pacific Railroad's shield shaped emblem has been in existence since 1886. Its yellow paint scheme has been used since the 1930s.

On December 31, 1925, Union Pacific Railroad operated 9,834 route miles; however, in 1982, the Union Pacific Railroad acquired the Missouri Pacific Railroad and Western Pacific Railroad followed by the Missouri–Kansas–Texas Railroad in 1988. Between 1926 and 1930, American Locomotive Company (Alco) built eighty-eight class 9000 steam locomotives with a 4-12-2 wheel arrangement and a top speed of 50 miles per hour. Weighing 495,000 pounds, this 102.58-foot-long locomotive had the longest rigid wheelbase of any United States steam locomotive. It was only used on the Union Pacific Railroad because its wheel arrangement could not negotiate tight curves that existed on many railroads. It was known as a type Union Pacific locomotive.

Alco built 105 Challenger type steam locomotives with a 4-6-6-4 wheel arrangement between 1936 and 1943. Weighing 627,900 pounds, the 122-foot-long locomotive had a maximum speed of 70 miles per hour. To climb the steep grade between Green River and Ogden, these locomotives required double heading and helper operation which slowed operation which prompted the introduction of the Big Boy. In 1941, Alco completed No. 4000 a 4-8-8-4 steam locomotive. After an Alco employee chalked the words "Big Boy" on the front of this locomotive, that designation was used for the twenty-five locomotives (Nos. 4000–4024) built for the Union Pacific during 1941 to 1944.

In December 1944, the Union Pacific Railroad received its last steam locomotive No. 844. This high-speed passenger locomotive handled trains such as the Overland Limited, Los Angeles Limited, and the Portland Rose. After diesel locomotives took over all of the Union Pacific Railroad passenger service, No. 844 handled freight service in Nebraska between 1957 and 1959. It was preserved for special service and became known as UP's living legend for its

excursion runs particularly between Laramie and Cheyenne, Wyoming, over Sherman Hill.

Between 1969 and 1971, Union Pacific Railroad purchased forty-seven type DD40X diesel locomotives from Electro-Motive Division of General Motors Corporation (EMD) (Nos. 6900–6946). These locomotives were named Centennial in honor of the Golden Spike Ceremony. With a weight of 545,000 pounds, the 98.41-foot-long 6,600-horsepower locomotive was the largest and most powerful diesel locomotive ever built with a top speed of 90 miles per hour. While these locomotives exhibited excellent performance and good efficiency, they were costly to maintain and were taken out of regular service by 1986.

By 1993, the Union Pacific Railroad had a 17,385-route mile system. UP merged with the Chicago & North Western Railway in April 1995. A merger with the Southern Pacific Company also included D&RGW and Cotton Belt. As noted by the Union Pacific Corporation Form 10-K Report for the fiscal year ended December 31, 2021, their rail network was 32,452 route miles plus 7,093 miles of other main lines, 3,412 miles of passing lines and turnouts, and 8,887 miles of switching and classification yard lines for a total of 51,844 miles compared to a total of 51,793 miles for December 31, 2020. As of December 31, 2021, the railroad owned or leased 7,242 multiple purpose locomotives, 158 switching locomotives, and seventy-six other locomotives for a total of 7,476 locomotives compared to a total of 8,721 for December 31, 2007. The railroad owned or leased 20,988 covered hopper cars, 5,925 open hopper cars, 8,139 gondola cars, 8,814 boxcars, 4,055 refrigerated cars, 3,399 flat cars, and 263 other cars for a total of 51,583 cars compared to a total of 94,284 cars for December 31, 2007.

Union Pacific Railroad's 2020 plan for the introduction of precision scheduled railroading (PSR) included: "Shifting the focus of operations from moving trains to moving cars; minimizing car dwell (time a car sits in the yard), car classification events and locomotive power requirements; utilizing general-purpose trains by blending existing train services; and balancing train movements to improve the utilization of crews and rail assets." However, concerns have been expressed over longer trains under PSR and the dramatic reduction of the railroad workforce. Union Pacific Railroad Form 10-K Reports show the operating ratio (operating expenses divided by operating revenues) decreased 27.9 percent from 79.3 percent in 2007 to 57.2 percent in 2021. Average number of UP employees decreased 40.3 percent from 50,100 in 2007 to 29,905 in 2021. Union Pacific Year 2021 Results report issued January 31, 2021 show workforce productivity was 1,038 car miles per employee, a 21.1 percent improvement compared to 857 car miles per employee in 2019. Average train length on a route measured in feet was 9,334 feet in 2021; a 17 percent increase compared 7,747 feet in 2019.

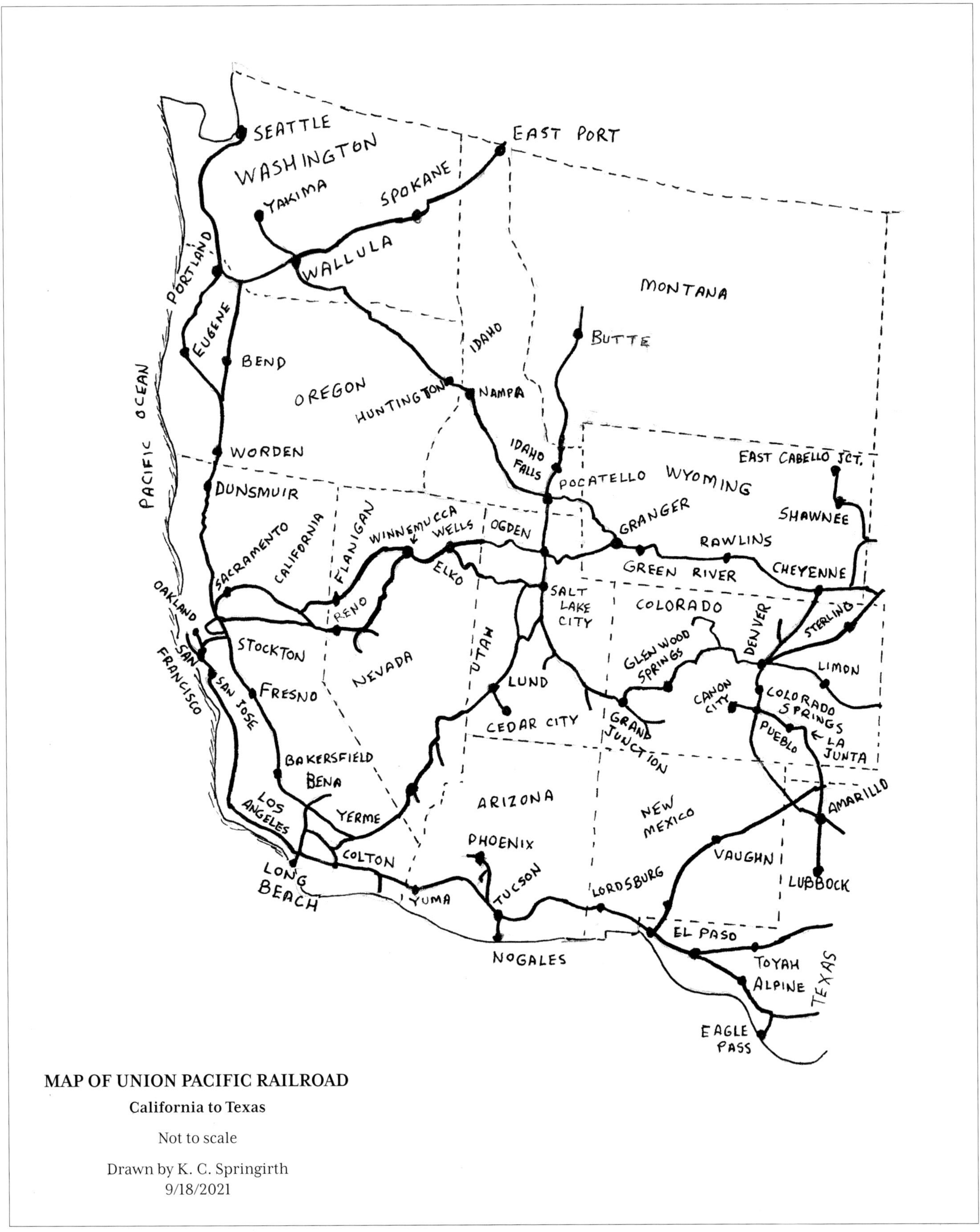

MAP OF UNION PACIFIC RAILROAD

California to Texas

Not to scale

Drawn by K. C. Springirth
9/18/2021

The California to Texas section of the Union Pacific Railroad is shown in the above map.

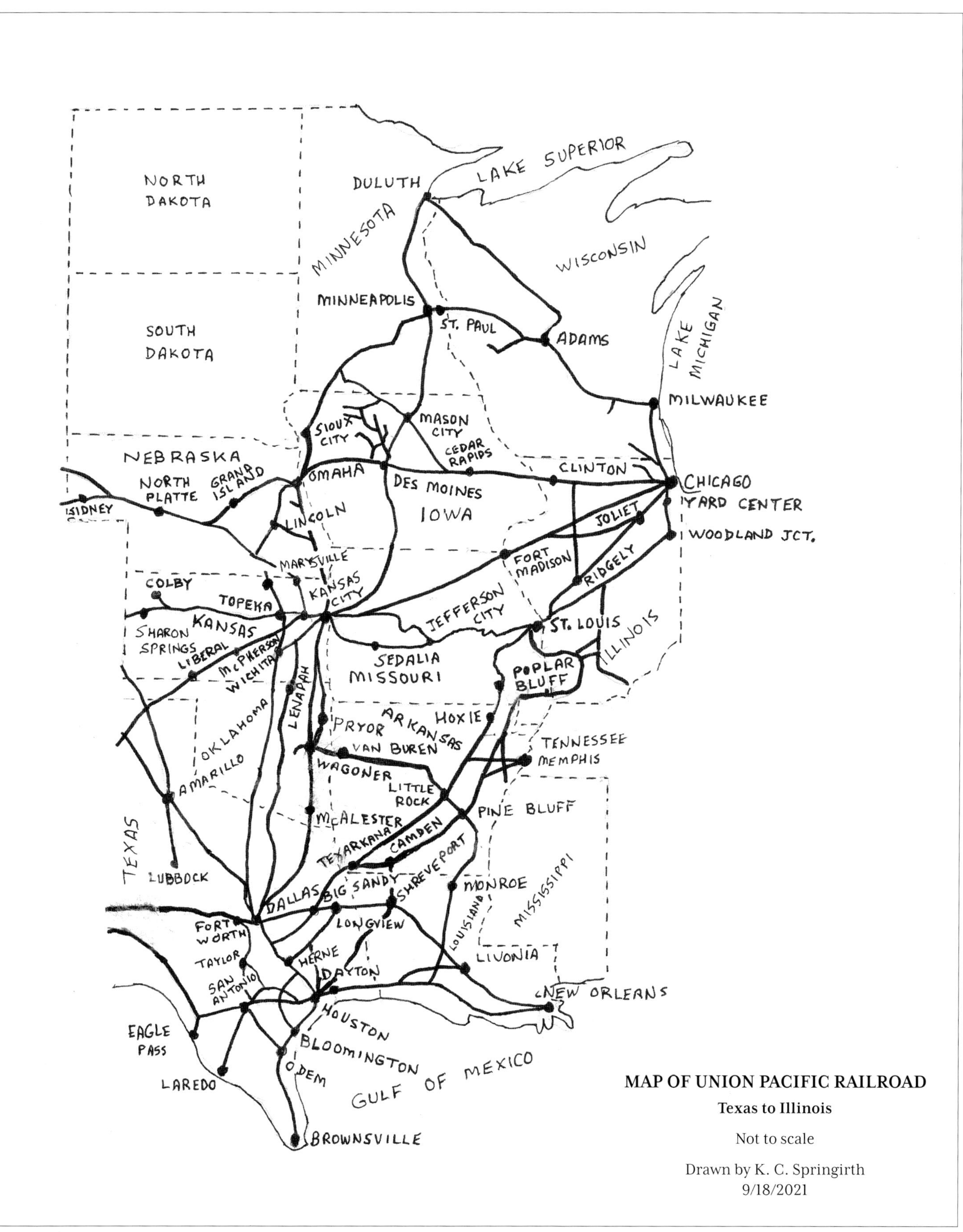

MAP OF UNION PACIFIC RAILROAD

Texas to Illinois

Not to scale

Drawn by K. C. Springirth
9/18/2021

The Texas to Illinois section of the Union Pacific Railroad is shown in the above map.

Union Pacific Railroad 5,500-horsepower locomotive No. 61 (Alco type Century 855 built in June 1964) in this postcard scene. Alco built three Century 855s that were used in the general freight pool based at North Platte, Nebraska. (*Alco Products Inc. Used with permission from Audio-Visual Designs [www.audiovisualdesigns.com]*)

The crew is boarding Union Pacific Railroad 1,750-horsepower EMD type F9A locomotive No. 522 (built as type F3A in January 1948 and rebuilt as F9AM in September 1958) heading a four-unit set for a timely departure in this June 1968 postcard. (*Photographer Mac Owen Used with permission from Audio-Visual Designs [www.audiovisualdesigns.com]*)

On September 2, 2021, Union Pacific Railroad four-axle 2,000-horsepower diesel locomotive No. 695 (EMD type GP38-2 built in February 1980 as No. 2195 for the Missouri Pacific Railroad) is trailing on an outbound grain train in Topeka, Kansas. (*Brian A. Keates photograph*)

The early morning of December 13, 2019 finds Union Pacific Railroad locomotive No. 831 (EMD type GP38-2 built in July 1981 as No. 2331 for the Missouri Pacific Railroad) crossing a road at the Topeka, Kansas, yard. (*Brian A. Keates photograph*)

On September 3, 2021, Union Pacific Railroad No. 1085 (four-axle 3,800-horsepower diesel electric locomotive type GP60 built in April 1991 by the Electro Motive Division of General Motors [EMD] originally as No. 9724 for the Southern Pacific Railroad) is trailing on an eastbound general manifest train. (*Brian A. Keates photograph*)

Topeka Yard is the location for four-axle 3,800-horsepower Union Pacific Railroad locomotive No. 1120 (GP60 built in February 1988 by EMD originally as No. 9608 for the Southern Pacific Railroad) switching cars in the Topeka, Kansas, yard on July 23, 2019. (*Brian A. Keates photograph*)

On September 1, 2021, Union Pacific Railroad No. 1383 (four-axle 3,000-horsepower GP40-2 built in February 1978 by EMD as No. 7627 for the Southern Pacific Railroad) is one of the locomotives powering an eastbound general manifest train at Topeka, Kansas. (*Brian A. Keates photograph*)

Union Pacific Railroad locomotive No. 1396 (GP40-2 built in January 1979 by EMD as No. 7640 for the St. Louis Southwestern Railway) is pulling an eastbound local freight out of the Topeka, Kansas, yard on September 1, 2021. (*Brian A. Keates photograph*)

In 1964, Union Pacific Railroad diesel electric freight locomotive No. 1638 (Alco 1,500-horsepower type FA with its matching B unit No. 1606) is at the city of Cheyenne in Laramie County, Wyoming, awaiting its next assignment. (*Photographer Mac Owen Used with permission from Audio-Visual Designs [www.audiovisualdesigns.com]*)

A westbound freight train is rolling through Topeka, Kansas, on September 2, 2021 powered by Union Pacific Railroad locomotive No. 2576 (Evolution series 4,400-horsepower type ET44AH built by GE in 2015). This was one of 200 ET44AH locomotives (Nos. 2570–2769) that met EPA Tier 4 emissions standards and ET meant they were heavier (432,000 pounds compared to the ES series standard of 416,000 pounds). (*Brian A. Keates photograph*)

A track inspection train headed by Union Pacific Railroad 4,400-horsepower GE type ET44AH locomotive No. 2612, built in 2015, is passing through Topeka, Kansas on August 11, 2019. (*Brian A. Keates photograph*)

Under a beautiful cloud formation in Topeka, Kansas, Union Pacific Railroad GE type ET44AH locomotive No. 2632, built in 2015, is powering an eastbound grain train on August 31, 2021. (*Brian A. Keates photograph*)

In Topeka, Kansas, on September 3, 2021, Union Pacific Railroad GE type ET44AH locomotive No. 2655, built in December 2015, is trailing on a westbound intermodal train. (*Brian A. Keates photograph*)

An eastbound Union Pacific Railroad train is passing through Topeka, Kansas, on December 11, 2019 with Distributed Power Unit (DPU) locomotive No. 2702 (GE type ET44AH built in 2016) in the middle of the train. A DPU is operated by remote control and is placed at the middle or end of a heavy train to help climb steep grades. (*Brian A. Keates photograph*)

On December 12, 2019, Union Pacific Railroad locomotive No. 2723 (GE type ET44AH built in September 2016) is leading a general manifest train across the Kansas River at Topeka, Kansas. (*Brian A. Keates photograph*)

Union Pacific Railroad locomotives No. 3977 (originally 4000-horsepower Southern Pacific No. 9803 built in July 1994 by EMD as type SD70M) and No. 695 (originally 2,000-horsepower Missouri Pacific Railroad No. 2195 built in February 1980 by EMD as type GP38-2) are trailing on a September 1, 2021 eastbound grain train at Topeka, Kansas. (*Brian A. Keates photograph*)

Union Pacific Railroad 4,000-horsepower No. 4199 (EMD type SD70M placed in service on August 18, 2000) is one of the units powering a southbound grain train passing through Topeka, Kansas, on September 2, 2021. (*Brian A. Keates photograph*)

On September 3, 2021, Union Pacific Railroad locomotive No. 5123 (EMD type SD70M went into service on October 14, 2002) is pulling a general manifest freight train southbound across the Kansas River at Topeka, Kansas. (*Brian A. Keates photograph*)

On September 1, 2021, Union Pacific Railroad (UP) six-axle 4,400-horsepower diesel locomotive No. 5411 (GE designation ES44AC, UP designation C45ACCTE placed in service March 29, 2005) is handling an intermodal train south across the Kansas River not far away from the Overland Station at Topeka, Kansas. This was an "Evolution Series" locomotive designed to meet the United States Environmental Protection Agency's Tier 2 locomotive emissions standards that took effect in 2005. (*Brian A. Keates photograph*)

Union Pacific Railroad locomotive No. 5430 (GE designation ES44AC, UP designation C45ACCTE placed in service on June 21 2005) is eastbound through Topeka, Kansas, on August 11, 2019. (*Brian A. Keates photograph*)

A general manifest train has crossed the Kansas River at Topeka, Kansas, on August 9, 2019 powered by Union Pacific Railroad 4,400-horsepower locomotive No. 5461 (GE designation ES44AC, UP designation C45ACCTE placed in service on June 16, 2005). (*Brian A. Keates photograph*)

On September 2, 2021, an eastbound general manifest freight train directed by Union Pacific Railroad 4,390-horsepower locomotive No. 5579 (GE designation type AC4400CW, UP designation C44ACCTE placed in service on September 10, 2004) with Canadian National Railways (CN) trailing locomotive No. 2862 (GE type ES44AC built in November 2013) is at Topeka, Kansas. (*Brian A. Keates photograph*)

A general manifest freight train is heading eastbound on August 6, 2019 out of the Topeka, Kansas, yard headed by Union Pacific Railroad locomotive No. 5640 (GE designation AC4400CW, UP designation C44ACCTE placed in service on November 8, 2004). (*Brian A. Keates photograph*)

Topeka, Kansas, is the location of Union Pacific Railroad locomotive No. 6290 on August 6, 2019. This originally was Southern Pacific Transportation Company locomotive No. 244 (GE designation AC4400AC; UP designation C44AC built in June 1995) known as a patch unit with the Union Pacific number patched over the original Southern Pacific locomotive paint scheme. (*Brian A. Keates photograph*)

Amid white puffy clouds, Union Pacific Railroad locomotive No. 6390 (GE designation AC4400CW; UP designation C44AC originally built in June 1995 as Southern Pacific No. 260) is pulling a northbound grain train across the Kansas River at Topeka, Kansas, on August 10, 2019. (*Brian A. Keates photograph*)

On August 10, 2019, Union Pacific Railroad 4,390-horsepower locomotive No. 6411 (GE designation AC4400CW; UP designation C44AC built in October 1995 for Southern Pacific as No. 365) is southbound preparing to cross the Kansas River at Topeka with an intermodal train. (*Brian A. Keates photograph*)

An eastbound Union Pacific Railroad locomotive No. 6468 (GE designation AC4400CW; UP designation C44AC built in July 2000) is leading an eastbound train through Topeka, Kansas, on August 7, 2019. (*Brian A. Keates photograph*)

Rear Distributed Power Unit No. 6618 (GE designation AC4400CW; UP designation C44ACCTE built in May 1997) for an empty westbound Union Pacific Railroad coal train is at Topeka, Kansas, on August 8, 2019. (*Brian A. Keates photograph*)

On September 1, 2021, a Union Pacific brakeman, with his yellow safety vest in compliance with Federal Railway Administration rules, is on the front of locomotive No. 6655 (GE designation AC4400CW UP designation C44ACCTE built in June 1997) deadheading to pick up the freight cars at the Topeka, Kansas yard. (*Brian A. Keates photograph*)

Union Pacific Railroad locomotive No. 6655 from the top of this page is now connected to the empty hopper cars at the Topeka, Kansas, yard on September 1, 2021. (*Brian A. Keates photograph*)

On September 1, 2021, Union Pacific Railroad locomotive No. 6718 (GE designation AC4400CW; UP designation C44AC built originally as No. 8816 in November 1994 for the Chicago & North Western Railway) is at the Topeka, Kansas, yard. (*Brian A. Keates photograph*)

Topeka, Kansas, on August 30, 2021, is the location of Union Pacific Railroad locomotive No. 6756 (GE designation AC4400CW; UP designation C44AC built in April 1996) powering an eastbound general manifest train. (*Brian A. Keates photograph*)

As the September 1, 2021 daylight fades into early evening, Union Pacific Railroad locomotive No. 6840 (GE designation AC4400CW; UP designation C44AC built in October 1995) is on a westbound run at Topeka, Kansas. (*Brian A. Keates photograph*)

Union Pacific Railroad locomotive No. 6900 (6,600-horsepower, making it the most powerful diesel electric locomotive ever built on a single frame and largest in the world weighing 545,000 pounds) after completion in April 1969 is on display in Salt Lake City, Utah for the 100th anniversary of the May 10, 1869 driving of the golden spike on at Promontory Summit, Utah. This 98.4-foot-long locomotive, equipped to run at 90 miles per hour, was one of forty-seven type DDA40X "Centennial" locomotives (Nos. 6900–6946) that resulted from a collaborative design between the railroad and builder EMD. High maintenance costs resulting from high in service mileage along with newer more reliable units (SD40-2 from EMD and C30-7 from GE) resulted in DDA40X locomotive No. 6936 making the last regular freight trip on May 6, 1985; however, this locomotive has been retained as part of the railroad's heritage fleet. (*Photographer Carl H. Sturner Used with permission from Audio-Visual Designs [www. audiovisualdesigns.com]*)

The mainline at Topeka, Kansas, yard on September 3, 2021, is the location of westbound Union Pacific Railroad locomotive No. 6998 (GE designation AC4400CW; UP designation C44AC built in September 1999). (*Brian A. Keates photograph*)

On September 3, 2021, Union Pacific Railroad locomotive No. 7102 (GE designation AC4400CW; UP designation A44AC built in June 1998) is at the Topeka, Kansas, yard on mainline trackage powering an eastbound train. It is truly amazing the number of freight trains that daily pass through this location. (*Brian A. Keates photograph*)

On September 1, 2021, Union Pacific Railroad locomotive No. 7146 (GE designation AC4400CW; UP designation C44AC built in April 1999) is powering a freight train near the Great Overland Station in Topeka, Kansas. (*Brian A. Keates photograph*)

The rear of a southbound train finds Union Pacific Railroad locomotive No. 7408 (GE designation ES44AC, UP designation C45ACCTE built in April 2009) functioning as a DPU on September 2, 2021. (*Brian A. Keates photograph*)

Union Pacific Railroad rear locomotive No. 7436 (GE designation ES44AC, UP designation C45ACCTE built in June 2009) is a DPU helper unit for this eastbound train on September 1, 2021. (*Brian A. Keates photograph*)

On September 1, 2021, Union Pacific Railroad locomotive No. 7702 (GE designation ES44AC, UP designation C45ACCTE built in June 2007) is at Topeka, Kansas. (*Brian A. Keates photograph*)

Westbound on the main line at the Topeka, Kansas, on September 2, 2021 is the location of Union Pacific Railroad locomotive No. 7704 (GE designation ES44AC; UP designation C45ACCTE built in June 2007). (*Brian A. Keates photograph*)

On September 2, 2021, Union Pacific Railroad locomotive No. 7843 (GE designation ES44AC; UP designation C45ACCTE built in March 2008) is pulling a special Federal Railroad Administration (FRA) inspection train at Topeka, Kansas. One of the responsibilities of the FRA (created by the Transportation Act of 1966) is to set track inspection standards. For example, if crossties of questionable condition are left in too long in track, the result could be a wide gauge derailment. (*Brian A. Keates photograph*)

The rest of the FRA inspection cars for the train on the bottom of page 52 are shown in this September 2, 2021 view. According to "Keeping the Union Pacific's Track Safe," the UP determines frequency by: "track classification, track type (main line, siding, or other track such as that found in a rail yard, million gross tons (MGT) amount of weight the train carries, type of traffic including hazmat and passenger, and weather conditions." (*Brian A. Keates photograph*)

On August 11, 2019 at 10:40 a.m., Union Pacific Railroad Geometry Car No. EC-4 is on the siding near Interstate 70 just past Ward Creek by Auburndale Park along the Kansas River in suburban Topeka, Kansas, waiting for the next assignment. The optical gauge measuring system, consisting of lasers and cameras, under the car evaluates track structure and tests for defects. (*Brian A. Keates photograph*)

Union Pacific Rail Inspection vehicle No. DC-64 is an example of the railroad's safety commitment. In addition to having track testing technology, the Union Pacific notes on their website *Keeping Union Pacific's Tracks Safe* "Most inspections are visual. An inspector walks or drives a hy-rail truck down the rails stopping regularly to measure the gauge or distance between the rails, as well as examine track conditions. Union Pacific uses special high tech equipment and inspection vehicles to look for internal defects not detectable by the human eye." (*Brian A. Keates photograph*)

There are two separate trains. Union Pacific Railroad eastbound 3,800-horsepower locomotive No. 1120 (GP60 built by EMD for Southern Pacific Railroad as No. 9608 in February 1988, became UP No. 5711 on April 26, 1999, UP No. 1911 on May 18, 2001, and later No. 1120) is a Distributed Power Unit on a local train. To the right No. 7937 (GE designation ES44AC, UP designation C45ACCTE built in April 2012) is on a general manifest train passing the local train on July 23, 2019 at Topeka, Kansas. (*Brian A. Keates photograph*)

On September 2, 2021, Union Pacific Railroad locomotive No. 7967 (GE designation ES44AC, UP designation C45ACCTE built in June 2012) is handling a southbound freight train at Topeka, Kansas. (*Brian A. Keates photograph*)

Topeka, Kansas, on September 2, 2021, is the location of a Union Pacific Railroad train headed by locomotive No. 8027 (GE designation ES44AC, UP designation C45ACCTE built in August 2012) (*Brian A. Keates photograph*)

A cloudy August 30, 2021 finds Union Pacific Railroad locomotive No. 8155 (GE type ES44AH built in May 2014) leading a freight train through Topeka, Kansas. (*Brian A. Keates photograph*)

From right to left: Union Pacific Railroad locomotives No. 8178 (GE type ES44AH built in 2014) and No. 5834 (GE designation AC4400CW, UP designation C44ACCTE built in March 2002) are at the Topeka, Kansas, yard on September 1, 2021. (*Brian A. Keates photograph*)

Union Pacific Railroad locomotive No. #8531 (six-axle 4,300-horsepower AC traction locomotive type SD70ACe delivered by EMD on June 16, 2007) is a DPU in the middle of a northbound train using the bridge crossing the Kansas River on August 30, 2021. The EMD SD70ACe was designed to meet EPA Tier 2 regulations. (*Brian A. Keates photograph*)

On August 30, 2021, a westbound Union Pacific Railroad train is at Topeka, Kansas, powered by locomotive No. 8612 (type SD70ACe delivered by EMD on July 12, 2007). (*Brian A. Keates photograph*)

Topeka, Kansas, on August 30, 2021 is the location of Union Pacific Railroad locomotive No. 8645 (EMD type SD70ACe built in June 2008). (*Brian A. Keates photograph*)

Union Pacific Railroad locomotive No. 8802 (EMD type SD70ACe built in 2013) is leading an eastbound freight train through Topeka, Kansas, on September 1, 2021. (*Brian A. Keates photograph*)

In September 2019, a westbound general manifest train at Topeka, Kansas, is headed by Union Pacific Railroad locomotive No. 8907 (EMD type SD70ACe built in 2014 that is designated by Union Pacific as an SD70AH with H for "heavy," because it is ballasted to 428,000 pounds instead of 420,000 pounds). (*Jacob A. Keates photograph*)

A southbound Union Pacific Railroad double stack intermodal train headed by locomotive No. 8976 (EMD type SD70AH built in 2014) is at the Topeka, Kansas, yard near the Kansas River on September 1, 2021. (*Brian A. Keates photograph*)

Two Union Pacific Railroad locomotives headed by No. 8985 (EMD type SD70AH built in 2014) are powering an eastbound coal train through the Topeka yard on September 1, 2021. (*Brian A. Keates photograph*)

On September 1, 2021, the Union Pacific mainline near Topeka, Kansas, is the location of an eastbound train headed by Union Pacific Railroad locomotive No. 9066 (EMD type SD70AH built in May 2017). (*Brian A. Keates photograph*)

2

Union Pacific Commemorative Locomotives

Union Pacific Railroad introduced a yellow paint scheme in 1934 noting the visibility of yellow would reduce grade crossing accidents. In 1941, Union Pacific Railroad began a yellow and gray paint scheme highlighted in red which is still used in 2021. The middle two-thirds of the locomotive body is painted Armour Yellow (color used by Armour & Company on their meat products packaging). A narrow band of Signal Red divides the Armour Yellow from the Harbor Mist Gray (light gray) used for the upper locomotive body and roof. Initially there was a thin band of Signal Red along the bottom of the locomotive body; however, this color has gradually become yellow as new Federal Railroad Administration regulations for reflectorized tape became effective in 2005. Locomotive trucks (painted Aluminum from 1955 to 1982), underframe, fuel tanks, and everything else below that line are Harbor Mist Gray. Locomotive lettering and numbering are in Signal Red with black outlines.

A number of railroads have been merged into the Union Pacific Railroad and have been commemorated by the following type SD70ACe locomotives: UP No. 1982 Missouri Pacific Railroad, UP No. 1983 Western Pacific Railroad, UP No. 1988 Missouri–Kansas–Texas Railroad, UP No. 1989 Denver & Rio Grande Western Railroad, UP No. 1995 Chicago & North Western Railroad, and UP No. 1996 Southern Pacific Railroad.

The Olympic Flame for the 2002 Olympic Winter Games traveled by train powered by UP type SD70M locomotives Nos. 2001 and 2002 with a special Cauldron Car for the Olympic Flame. Community service locomotives include Union Pacific Railroad type SD70AH locomotive No. 9026, that was shipped to National Railway Equipment at Mt. Vernon, Illinois, where it was sandblasted, primed, repainted, renumbered No. 1943, and was unveiled at San Antonio's Sunset Station on October 19, 2017 and began a Salute to the Military Tour across Union Pacific's railroad system. UP locomotive type SD70ACe No. 4141 was a tribute to former President George Herbert Walker Bush.

On February 16, 2020, Union Pacific Railroad locomotive No. 1111, "Powered by our people" just under the cab window (highlighting the company's skilled employees who achieve the theme "We can handle it") is heading a freight train at Morrilton, the county seat of Conway County, Arkansas. The number 1111, unveiled on June 6, 2019, represents Union Pacific's goal to be the No. 1 railroad with the No. 1 employees who have the No. 1 safety dedication with one vision—Building America. This locomotive was originally No. 8362 (EMD type SD70ACe delivered on June 3, 2005). (*John Bryan photograph*)

On July 28, 2021, Union Pacific Railroad "Employee Pride Locomotive" No. 1111 is rounding the curve at Fort Worth, Texas. According to the Union Pacific Building America website, "Twelve employees at Union Pacific's Jenks Shop in North Little Rock, Arkansas blasted, sanded, striped, painted, and decaled the Employee Pride Locomotive." (*Dylan Chastain photograph*)

On May 31, 2018, Union Pacific Railroad locomotive No. 1943 leads the executive train through the borough of Topton in Berks County, Pennsylvania, honoring a B-17F Flying Fortress bomber that was shot down while the plane was on a bombing mission over Münster, Germany. The locomotive was painted to honor veterans from all branches of military service with Air Force Silver, followed by the Coast Guard's racing stripe, the Navy's Battleship Gray, camo for the Army and Marines, and the POW/MIA symbol. This locomotive was originally No. 9026 (EMD type SD70AH built in 2016 (*Brian A. Keates photograph*)

Union Pacific Railroad No. 1982, Missouri Pacific heritage locomotive, is passing through the city of Mayflower in Faulkner County, Arkansas, on October 5, 2018. This locomotive (originally Union Pacific No. 8379 EMD type SD70ACe built in 2005 was renumbered 1982 and repainted July 16, 2005) features a two-tone blue and white paint scheme that pays tribute to the Missouri Pacific's passenger train streamliner days and the eagle graphic of the front of the locomotive that implies power and speed. On January 1, 1997, Missouri Pacific Railroad was merged into the Union Pacific Railroad. (*John Bryan photograph*)

On January 3, 2021, at the town of Chico in Wise County, Texas, this frontal view shows Union Pacific's heritage locomotive No. 1982 commemorating Missouri Pacific's 1940s blue, gray, and white paint scheme. Not visible is Missouri Pacific's solid dark blue 1960s paint scheme in the rear of the locomotive. (*Dylan Chastain photograph*)

Union Pacific Railroad No. 1983, Western Pacific Railroad heritage locomotive, is one of the diesel units powering a freight train over a bridge across the Arkansas River at Conway, county seat of Faulkner County, Arkansas, on July 10, 2020. Locomotive No. 1983 was originally Union Pacific Railroad locomotive No. 8383 (EMD type SD70ACe built in 2005) and was renumbered to 1983 on July 16, 2005. In 1949, the Western Pacific, Denver & Rio Grande Western, and Chicago Burlington & Quincy together introduced a new streamlined passenger train "California Zephyr" between Chicago and Oakland. The Union Pacific Railroad acquired the Western Pacific Railroad on December 22, 1982. (*John Bryan photograph*)

On September 10, 2021, Union Pacific Railroad locomotive No. 1983 commemorating the Western Pacific heritage paint scheme (solid green with orange lettering in 1970 followed by an orange nose in 1979) is heading a freight train in Fort Worth, Texas. The Western Pacific operated in California, Nevada, and Utah with its main line paralleling Southern Pacific between Oakland and Salt Lake City. (*Dylan Chastain photograph*)

On April 2, 2021, the bridge over the muddy Arkansas River at Conway, Arkansas, is the location of Union Pacific Railroad heritage locomotive numbered 1988 (originally Union Pacific Railroad No. 8396 EMD type SD70ACe built in May 2005 was renumbered to 1988 on August 17, 2005 commemorating the year the Missouri Kansas Texas Railroad, known as the Katy, was acquired), and Union Pacific Railroad helper locomotive No. 6203 (GE type AC4400CW originally Southern Pacific Railroad No. 188 built May 1995 and renovated on April 24, 2008) are powering a freight train. The Katy added six Midwestern states and 3,377 miles of track to the Union Pacific Railroad. (*John Bryan photograph*)

Union Pacific Railroad heritage locomotive "The Katy" No. UP 1988 (originally No. 8396 EMD type SD70ACe built in May 2005 and renumbered to 1988 on August 17, 2005) along with Union Pacific Railroad locomotive No. 6898 (originally 6,000-horsepower No. 7510 GE type AC6000CW built in July 1998 that was repowered and rerated to 4,350-horsepower power type and reclassified C44/60AC by UP) plus another UP locomotive are passing under a highway bridge at Conway, Arkansas, on April 2, 2021. Headquartered in Dallas, Texas, the Katy had operating centers in Denison, Texas; Bellmead, Texas; and Parsons, Kansas. It served as an important north-south link connecting the Midwest with Texas. (*John Bryan photograph*)

Under a cloudy bright Arkansas sky at Conway, Arkansas, on August 31, 2020, Union Pacific heritage locomotive featuring the historic colors of the Denver & Rio Grande Western Railroad No. 1989 (originally UP No. 8521 EMD type SD70ACe delivered on May 24, 2006 in primer and renumbered to 1989 on June 8, 2006) and helper Union Pacific No. 5846 (GE designation AC4400CW; UP designation C44ACCTE placed in service on May 15, 2002) are powering a coal train. With the opening of the Moffat Tunnel on February 26, 1928, the Denver & Rio Grande Western's Denver–Salt Lake Route was shortened, and the railroad became known as the Scenic Line of the World. (*John Bryan photograph*)

On August 29, 2020, Union Pacific Railroad No. 1989 is powering a coal train passing the Morrilton, Arkansas former Missouri Pacific train station located on Railroad Avenue between Division and Moose Streets which last saw passenger service on March 28, 1960. The December 16, 1951 *Official Guide of the Railways* showed the *Rainbow Special* on its 1,011.7-mile Kansas City–New Orleans route stopped at Morrilton at 10:40 a.m. southbound and 5:04 p.m. northbound. The single-story brick building with a tile roof has styling typical of Missouri Pacific passenger stations. (*John Bryan photograph*)

On February 10, 2020, Union Pacific Railroad heritage locomotive No. 1995 honoring the Chicago Northwestern originally UP No. 8522 (EMD type SD70ACe was delivered on June 17, 2006 in primer and was renumbered to 1995 on July 11, 2006) is heading a train through Conway, Arkansas. This was the fifth unit in the UP heritage fleet and was introduced at Chicago's Ogilvie Transportation Center on July 15, 2006. The Chicago & Northwestern served Chicago commuters, Michigan iron ore mines, and Illinois coal fields with a network of branch lines in the MidweSt. (*John Bryan photograph*)

On November 10, 2021, Union Pacific Railroad's Chicago & Northwestern Railroad heritage locomotive No. 1995 is at Chico, Texas. The Chicago & North Western was the first railroad to connect with the Union Pacific at Council Bluffs in 1867, and partnered with Union Pacific in 1984 to open a railroad line to Wyoming's Powder River Basin coal fields. Chicago & North Western Railway merged into Union Pacific Railroad on June 23, 1995. (*Dylan Chastain photograph*)

Little Rock, Arkansas, on October 23, 2019 is the location of Union Pacific Railroad's Southern Pacific Transportation Company heritage locomotive No. 1996 originally No. 8523 (EMD type SD70ACe delivered on June 24, 2006 in primer and renumbered 1996 on August 7, 1996). This locomotive features historic colors that honor the employees of that former railroad and was inspired by their famous "Daylight" trains that were often characterized as "The Most Beautiful Trains in the World." (*John Bryan photograph*)

On October 23, 2019, Union Pacific Railroad's smartly painted Southern Pacific Transportation Company locomotive No. 1996 is helping a freight train across the Arkansas River at Conway, Arkansas. Over the years, the Southern Pacific Transportation Company expanded to a 13,000-mile system that extensively served southwestern United States. The Southern Pacific Transportation Company merged with the Union Pacific Railroad on September 11, 1996. (*John Bryan photograph*)

Mayflower, Faulkner County, Arkansas, on November 7, 2019 is the location of Union Pacific Railroad special painted Olympic Torch Relay locomotive No. 2001 (originally EMD No. 4690 type SD70M built in August 2001) with No. 8136 (GE type ES44AH built in March 2014) behind it. This was one of two specially painted Union Pacific locomotives Nos. 2001 and 2002 that pulled a specially designed train for the 2002 Olympic Games in Salt Lake City and the 2002 Olympic Torch Relay with a uniquely created Cauldron Car for the Olympic flame. (*John Bryan photograph*)

Special painted Union Pacific Railroad locomotive No. 2001 with Union Pacific Railroad helper locomotive No. 4829 (EMD type SD70M placed in service on August 29, 2002) is crossing a bridge over the Arkansas River at Conway, Arkansas, on November 7, 2019. (*John Bryan photograph*)

On February 18, 2019, North Little Rock, Arkansas, is the location of Union Pacific Railroad locomotive No. 4141 (originally No. 8423 EMD type SD70ACe built in July 2005 was renumbered to 4141 on October 7, 2005) honoring President George Herbert Walker Bush. Weighing 420,000 pounds with a full tank of diesel fuel, this 4,300-horsepower locomotive has a maximum speed of 70 miles per hour. On the right is Union Pacific No. 5222 (EMD 4,000 horsepower type SD70M placed in service on December 29, 2004). (*John Bryan photograph*)

Union Pacific Railroad No. 4141 (in honor of the forty-first president) George Bush Locomotive is at North Little Rock, Arkansas, on February 18, 2019. According to the Union Pacific Railroad Building America website, "The UP No. 4141 George Bush Locomotive was unveiled October 18, 2005, during a ceremony near the George Bush Presidential Library and Museum on the Texas A&M University campus in College Station, Texas." On December 6, 2018, locomotive No. 4141 along with No. 1943 "The Spirit" were in Bush's funeral train running from Spring to College Station, Texas. (*John Bryan photograph*)

3

Union Pacific's Big Boy Locomotives

The National Defense Act during 1940 encouraged railroads to develop more powerful locomotives to handle wartime requirements. Designed by the mechanical department of the Union Pacific Railroad (UP), American Locomotive Company (Alco) of Schenectady, New York, in close collaboration with UP built twenty-five Big Boy locomotives (twenty—Nos. 4000–4019—each costing $265,174 in 1941 and five—Nos. 4020–4024—each costing $319,600 in 1944) for the UP with the first one delivered on September 4, 1941. It was designed to reach speeds of 80 miles per hour, handle a maximum curvature of 20 degrees, and produce maximum power at 30 to 40 miles per hour. As noted in *The Big Legacy of the Union Pacific Big Boy* by James J. Reisdorff and Michael M. Bartels, "Under full steam it consumed 100,000 pounds of water and 22,000 pounds of coal per hour." These 4000 series locomotives handled the steep terrain between Ogden, Utah, and Cheyenne, Wyoming. The approximately 7,000-horsepower Big Boy locomotive was 132.82 feet long over couplers, weighed 1.2 million pounds, had a maximum tractive power of 135,375 pounds, and had a 4-8-8-4 wheel arrangement which meant four wheels on the leading set of pilot wheels which guided the engine, eight drivers, another set of eight drivers, and four wheels following which supported the rear of the locomotive. The first twenty Big Boy locomotives had seven-axle Centipede tenders that had a capacity of 24,000 gallons of water and 28 tons of coal. The final batch of five tenders had a 25,000 gallon water capacity. During the time the locomotives were built, the UP rebuilt bridges, installed 130-pound rail from Ogden to the summit at Wahsatch, increased curve radii where possible, and adjusted track centers to make sure Big Boy locomotives had adequate clearance for passing trains. In areas where it was not possible to ease curves, passing and meet restrictions were established.

In December 1941, Big Boy No. 4014 was delivered to the Union Pacific Railroad. Initially Big Boy locomotives operated between Ogden and Green River; however, during World War II these locomotives operated east to Rawlins, Laramie, and Cheyenne. In the 1950s, an increasing number of diesels on the Union Pacific Railroad meant less work for steam locomotives. On the evening of July 20, 1959, No. 4014 made its last revenue trip from Laramie via Sherman Hill arriving at Cheyenne in the early morning of July 21, 1959. Having traveled 1,031,205 miles in twenty years of service, it was retired in December 1961. Steam locomotives were phased out because of more economical diesel locomotives. UP saved eight of the 4000 series locomotives and donated them for display. In 2013, UP reacquired No. 4014 from the Rail Giants Museum in Pomona, California, where over the years volunteers removed ash and cinders from the firebox, cleaned plus painted gauges, rewired the engine for lighting, made a sheet metal cover to keep rainwater from entering the smokebox, installed pistons in the cylinders, kept the engine oiled plus greased, and repainted the locomotive. That work made No. 4014 the leading candidate for restoration. It was positioned on a train between Union Pacific Railroad type SD70M diesels Nos. 4884 and 4014 that left California on April 28, 2014 and travelled via Los Vegas, Nevada; Ogden, Utah; and arrived at Cheyenne, Wyoming, on May 8, 2014 where it was restored. No. 4014 is the only operating Big Boy in the world. On May 9, 2019, No. 4014 made a trip to Ogden, Utah, to commemorate the 150th anniversary of the completion of America's first transcontinental railroad.

Seven Other Big Boy Locomotives have been Preserved

No. 4004 is at Holliday Park E. 19th & Morrie Avenue, Cheyenne, Wyoming. Built in September 1941, this locomotive had a lifetime mileage of 1,060,402 and was retired in February 1962.

No. 4005 is at Forney Museum of Transportation 4303 Brighton Boulevard, Denver, Colorado. Built in September 1941, this locomotive had a lifetime mileage of 1,043,624 and was retired in July 1962.

No. 4006 is at the Museum of Transportation 2933 Barrett Station Road, St. Louis, Missouri. Built in September 1941, this locomotive had a lifetime mileage of 1,064,625 (highest mileage of the twenty-five Big Boy locomotives) and was retired in May 1961.

No. 4012 is at the Steamtown National Historic Site 350 Cliff Street, Scranton, Pennsylvania. Built in November 1941, this locomotive had a lifetime mileage of 1,029,507 and was retired in February 1962.

No. 4017 is at the National Railroad Museum 2285 South Broadway, Green Bay, Wisconsin. Built in December 1941, this locomotive had a lifetime mileage of 1,052,072 and was retired in May 1961.

No. 4018 is at the Museum of the American Railroad 800 N. Dallas Parkway, Frisco, Texas. Built in December 1941, this locomotive had a lifetime mileage of 1,037,123 and was retired in July 1962.

No. 4023 is at Kenefick Park (named for former Union Pacific Railroad Chairman and CEO John C. Kenefick) in Lauritzen Gardens 100 Bancroft Street, Omaha, Nebraska. Built in November 1944, this locomotive had a lifetime mileage of 829,295 and was retired in July 1962.

The total lifetime mileage of the eight saved Union Pacific Big Boy locomotives is 8,147,853 miles.

A special excursion in June 1968 finds Union Pacific Railroad 4-8-4 Northern type steam locomotive No. 8444 in Yoder, Goshen County, Wyoming. This was originally No. 844 which was one of ten locomotives Nos. 835-844 built in 1944 by Alco in Schenectady, New York. For a while, this locomotive was renumbered 8444 to distinguish it from a diesel numbered in the 800 series; however, it regained its No. 844 in June 1969, after the diesel was retired. Alco built twenty (Nos. 800–819) in 1937 and fifteen (Nos. 820-834) in 1939. All forty-five of these locomotives were built with a cast steel frame replacing many separate parts by one single casting which facilitated maintenance. That feature was applied to the Big Boy locomotives. (*Photographer Mac Owen Used with permission from Audio-Visual Designs [www.audiovisualdesigns.com]*)

Superpower is on display at Cheyenne, Wyoming, in this November 1956 postcard scene for two freight trains ready for the push over Sherman Hill. The train on the left is headed by 4,500-horsepower gas turbine locomotive No. 75. The first ten UP gas turbine locomotives (Nos. 51–60) were 4,500 horsepower delivered by General Electric Company (GE) in 1952 with an additional fifteen more (Nos. 61–75) ordered from GE in 1954. The locomotive on the right is Big Boy No. 4022, built by Alco in November 1944, which like the other twenty-four Big Boys paid dividends on their investment; however, they were replaced by more economical diesels after July 21, 1959. (*Photographer Douglas C. Wornom Used with permission from Audio-Visual Designs [www.audiovisualdesigns.com]*)

Union Pacific Railroad Big Boy No. 4004 is at the city of Laramie in Albany County, Wyoming, on October 16, 1955. Completed in September 1941, this was the fifth locomotive of the first order of twenty Union Pacific 4-8-8-4s completed by Alco's Schenectady, New York, plant. (*Photographer Bob Collins Used with permission from Audio-Visual Designs [www.audiovisualdesigns.com]*)

It is full speed ahead as Union Pacific Railroad Big Boy steam locomotive No. 4014 passes over the flat rural area lof Kansas in August 2019. On the parallel highway, people parked their automobiles along the highway to observe and photograph this amazing locomotive. Following a massive restoration process, this locomotive returned to service following the May 9, 2019 ceremony at Ogden, Utah, commemorating the 150th anniversary commemorating the completion of the transcontinental railroad. (*Beth Anne Keates photograph*)

Union Pacific Railroad crew members do an inspection of Big Boy No. 4014 on August 5, 2019, at the same time the public gets a view of the locomotive at North Platte, Nebraska. This marked the beginning of its first tour detailed by the June 13, 2019 Union Pacific News Release which noted the locomotive would be on display in the following cities: July 13–14: Omaha, Nebraska; July 18: St. Paul, Minnesota; July 20: Duluth, Minnesota; July 23: Altoona, Wisconsin; July 27–29: West Chicago, Illinois; August 1: Des Moines, Iowa; August 3: Omaha, Nebraska; and August 6; North Platte, Nebraska. (*Andrew L. Keates photograph*)

The August 5, 2019 arrival of Union Pacific Railroad Big Boy No. 4014 at North Platte, Nebraska, is greeted by many wanting to view this locomotive. Later in the summer a September 5, 2019 Union Pacific News Release noted the locomotive would be on display in the following cities: October 2–3: Provo, Utah; October 7: Las Vegas, Nevada; October 10–11: Greater Los Angeles, California; October 18: Tucson, Arizona; and October 21–22: El Paso, Texas. (*Andrew L. Keates photograph*)

While spectators at Kansas City are focused on UP Big Boy No. 4014, a general manifest freight train is passing by powered by two Union Pacific diesel locomotives, each displaying the United States flag, on August 31, 2021. This is the only operating Big Boy locomotive in the world. Union Pacific donated seven other Big Boy locomotives to museums or parks in the United States. Hence eight of the twenty-five Big Boy locomotives or 32 percent have been preserved. That represents the largest number of articulated locomotives from one railroad to be preserved in North America. (*Andrew L. Keates photograph*)

On August 31, 2021, a five diesel unit Burlington Northern Santa Fe Railway intermodal train is passing the Big Boy attraction at Kansas City. The Big Boy locomotive was recognized for its ability to handle long heavy freight trains across the Wasatch mountain range between Green River, Wyoming, and Ogden, Utah. (*Andrew L. Keates photograph*)

A daytime August 31, 2021 view of Union Pacific Railroad Big Boy 4014 from the roof top of the parking lot in Kansas City, Missouri, shows many who came to experience this historic event. The Union Pacific Railroad June 14, 2021 News Release noted that the locomotive would leave the Steam Shop in Cheyenne, Wyoming, August 5 and be on display in the following cities: August 14: Fort Worth, Texas; August 17: Houston, Texas; August 21: New Orleans, Louisiana; August 29: St. Louis, Missouri: and September 6: Denver, Colorado. (*Andrew L. Keates photograph*)

On August 31, 2021 at the Kansas City stop, the line-up of traffic cones is a reminder to the public to avoid getting too close to the Union Pacific Big Boy. (*Andrew L. Keates photograph*)

The arrival of early evening on August 31, 2021 still finds people (excited about steam locomotive No. 4014) at Kansas City Union Station enthralled by this unique opportunity to witness an important aspect of our nation's rail heritage. The locomotive was not on tour in 2020 because of the pandemic. This is a tremendous piece of history that contributed to the rail heritage of the United States. By design a portion of a steam engine's parts are visible which is fascinating and esthetically pleasing to view. (*Andrew L. Keates photograph*)

Since a steam locomotive trip is a logistical challenge, every stop is an opportunity for Union Pacific employees to make sure that Big Boy No. 4014 is kept is excellent condition as seen in this August 31, 2021 view. (*Andrew L. Keates photograph*)

Union Pacific Railroad Big Boy No. 4014 passes a crossing at Rossville in Shawnee County, Kansas, that is part of the Topeka, Kansas, Metropolitan Statistical Area on September 2, 2021. For drivers and pedestrians, the September 23, 2019 Union Pacific News Release noted the following rail safety tips: "Only cross the tracks at designated railroad crossings, located where the street intersects with the tracks; Never walk between the rails or in areas that are not designated crossings; Avoid distractions including loud music, texting, or talking on cell phones when crossing the railroad tracks; and stay away from trains and other railroad property including bridges, yards and other equipment." (*Brian A. Keates photograph*)

On September 1, 2021, Union Pacific Railroad Big Boy No. 4014 crosses a big bridge coming out of Kansas City while a Burlington Northern Santa Fe Railway freight train is travelling underneath the bridge. (*Brian A. Keates photograph*)

Union Pacific Railroad Big Boy No. 4014 with helper diesel locomotive No. 4015, three tenders behind, is northbound near the city of North Platte, county seat of Lincoln, Nebraska, on August 9, 2019 pulling this huge special train. (*Andrew L. Keates photograph*)

On September 2, 2021 at Rossville, Kansas, helper diesel locomotive No. 4015 (EMD type SD70M placed in service on July 25, 2000) is an important component in Union Pacific Railroad's Big Boy's special train, because it gives the steam locomotive a longer distance between fuel and water stops plus serves as a switcher locomotive when the train has to be broken up for overnight storage or display. This locomotive burns used engine oil instead of coal. (*Brian A. Keates photograph*)

On August 6, 2019, a group of people are at this crossing to look and admire Union Pacific Railroad Big Boy No. 4014. The Union Pacific September 21, 2020 News Release noted, "Every five days a child dies as a result of a train collision, and approximately every three hours a vehicle or pedestrian is struck on the tracks." That news release also noted that walking near or on the tracks is against the law, and trains can overhang tracks by at least three feet. Cross tracks only at locations where there is a crossbuck, lights, or gates; however, look both ways before crossing tracks. When lights are flashing and or gates are down, wait for the train to pass. Never try to beat the train, because it can take up to a mile to stop. (*Andrew L. Keates photograph*)

A close view of Union Pacific Railroad Big Boy No. 4014 at a rural crossing creates an exciting scene just outside of Kansas City, Kansas, on September 2, 2021. (*Brian A. Keates photograph*)

Under the beautiful blue sky of August 6, 2019, Union Pacific Railroad Big Boy No. 4014 has some grain silos behind it north of the North Platte, Nebraska, railroad yard. On a fabulous summer day, this was the start of the first season of the Union Pacific Railroad Big Boy steam locomotive tour. (*Beth Anne Keates photograph*)

In North Platte, Nebraska, on August 6, 2019, Union Pacific Railroad Big Boy No. 4014 attracts people photographing trains. The Union Pacific June 14, 2021 News Release noted: "Weighing in at 1.2 million pounds, the Big Boy makes a big impression in communities it visits, reminding us of bygone days and the important role the railroad continues to play in our global economy," said Scott Moore, senior vice president—corporate relations and chief administrative officer. (*Andrew L. Keates photograph*)

In the summer of 1971, Steamtown (at the village of Bellows Falls in Windham County, Vermont) features in the cab of Union Pacific Railroad Big Boy locomotive No. 4012. *From left to right*: Laurel, Robyn, and at age three Robert A. Elder. This trip to Steamtown nurtured Robert's interest in trains that has resulted in him in 2022 operating the Tunnel Inn in Gallitzin, Pennsylvania where his inn has fulfilled his dream of making it possible for people of all ages to experience the wonderful hobby of rail transportation. In 1984, Steamtown moved to Scranton, Pennsylvania. (R.M. Elder, photograph)

In 2008, Union Pacific Railroad Big Boy No. 4012 (before being repainted) is at Steamtown in Scranton, Pennsylvania, sitting on a prime display track easily viewable by visitors pulling in to visit the park. Francis Nelson Blount (May 21, 1918–August 31, 1967), founder of Blount Seafood Corporation and founder of Steamtown, USA, discovered that to acquire this locomotive, it had to be in the name of a not-for-profit organization. He established Steamtown USA as a not-for-profit organization in Bellows Falls, Vermont. Union Pacific Railroad donated No. 4012 to Steamtown which later moved to Scranton, Pennsylvania. The National Parks Service acquired Steamtown in 1995. (*Bob Elder photograph*)

4

Great Overland Station
Topeka, Kansas

Great Overland Station in Topeka, Kansas, designed by architect Gilbert Stanley Underwood, was a Union Pacific Railroad passenger station that opened on January 27, 1927. Almost 20,000 people attended the station's grand opening, and the station was considered one of the largest and finest stations west of the Missouri River. The station was inundated by the Great Flood of July 13, 1951 which rose more than eight feet and caused extensive interior damage. Passengers using the station declined through the 1950s and 1960s. After the last passenger train left the station on May 2, 1971, the Union Pacific Railroad used the station for office space and a customer service center until vacating the building in 1989. A fire damaged the western part of the station in 1992. That same year Railroad Heritage Inc. (a nonprofit corporation with a goal to preserve Topeka's railroad history plus significant history of the region) agreed to renovate and rehabilitate the station. In 1998, Union Pacific Railroad donated the station to Railroad Heritage Inc. Today that restored station with its soaring ceilings and magnificent design provides a beautiful setting for visitors as a museum and a perfect venue for a multitude of events. On October 1, 2002, the Great Overland Station was added to the National Register of Historic Places.

This is an overall view of the Great Overland Station located at 701 N. Kansas Avenue in Topeka, Kansas, on September 3, 2021. The station is a beautiful Classical Revival style which is characterized by a symmetrical design for doors plus rectangular windows and features a center pavilion with two smaller pavilions on each side. Adding to this scene are the nicely placed flags. (*Brian A. Keates photograph*)

A view from the side on a beautiful September 3, 2021 shows the magnificent architecture of the Great Overland Station. (*Brian A. Keates photograph*)

A close up view shows the unique design of the Great Overland Station on September 3, 2021. (*Brian A. Keates photograph*)

An August 8, 2019 view, after renovations of the station were completed, shows the beautiful interior of the Great Overland Station with its soaring ceilings and intricate ornamentation. As one walks thru the interior, imagine how many people sat in the waiting room, ate a meal, and hopped a train to another destination. Also pause to remember all of the military personnel who passed through the station on their way to war, with many of them paying the ultimate sacrifice. (*Brian A. Keates photograph*)

All of the beautiful colors of the interior have been meticulously restored to match the original style of the Great Overland Station in this August 8, 2019 scene. (*Brian A. Keates photograph*)

Union Pacific Railroad locomotive No. 3893 (EMD type SD70M placed in service March 7, 2003) and No. 4382 (EMD type SD70M placed in service on May 25, 2001) are ready to pass the Great Overland Station in Topeka, Kansas, on September 3, 2021. (*Brian A. Keates photograph*)

On September 3, 2021, Union Pacific Railroad locomotive No. 7308 (GE designation AC6000 convertible (designated convertible because this type of locomotive was originally supposed to be converted to 6,250 horsepower); Union Pacific designation C44/60AC built in May 1998) is at the trailing end of a freight train passing the Great Overland Station. (*Brian A. Keates photograph*)

5

Union Pacific Railroad Bailey Yard, North Platte, Nebraska

North Platte, a Lincoln County city in the west-central part of Nebraska, is the location of Bailey Yard, the world's largest classification yard. North Platte was planned as a railroad town by chief engineer Grenville Dodge because of the nearby availability of good water, and the town received its first train in 1866. Major shop facilities and winter quarters for train crews were constructed at North Platte. Main line operations began through North Platte in 1867, and the early yard was flat switched with twenty tracks. North Platte became a UP division point where trains are sorted, railroad crews exchanged, and maintenance or repairs are made on equipment. In 1948, Bailey Yard (named after former Union Pacific Railroad president Edd H. Bailey [1965–1971]) became a hump yard with forty-two tracks. A sixty-four-track hump yard was added in 1968 followed by a diesel locomotive shop in 1971, and a railroad car shop in 1974. The 1948 hump yard was replaced by a fifty-track yard in 1980. Train operations and repair shops at Bailey Yard are open twenty-four hours a day, seven days a week. The yard has an in-motion wheel defect detector developed by UP that uses ultrasound technology to inspect each wheel. At Bailey Yard, trains are either broken up and reclassified, or serviced, inspected, and sent on their way.

The September 1, 2020 *North Platte Telegraph* newspaper noted the UP announcement, "Union Pacific will begin operating Bailey Yard as a single classification yard, due to improved customer shipment processing times. All rail shipments will be sorted on the west side of Bailey Yard, which plays a critical role on the Union Pacific network. The changes are a testament to the team's operational excellence and safe, reliable service to customers. We do not anticipate changes at Bailey Yard will have a significant impact on the estimated 1,600 employees who are based in North Platte." Actually this was part of the UP plan for implementing Precision Scheduled Railroading shifting the focus of operations from moving trains to moving cars plus minimizing car dwell, car classification events, and locomotive power requirements.

This is an August 6, 2019 view of the Golden Spike Tower and Visitor Center that opened on June 26, 2008 to allow visitors to get a view of Bailey Yard at North Platte, Nebraska. (*Beth Anne Keates* photograph)

From the top of the Golden Spike Tower, there is a wonderful view of the massive 2,850-acre, 8-mile-long and 2-mile-wide Bailey Yard on August 6, 2019. (*Beth Anne Keates photograph*)

In this August 6, 2019 view, there are a large number of locomotives and freight cars at Bailey Yard. (*Beth Anne Keates photograph*)

6

Union Pacific Railroad Diesel Locomotive Pooling

t is common to see a train from one railroad which is powered partly or entirely by locomotives from another railroad. Railroads are able to exchange trains without exchanging locomotives which saves time and money. A deal between two railroads to share locomotives, is known as a pooled power agreement. If the locomotive operates on another railroad or multiple railroads without stopping, it is called "run-through power." In most cases, it is more efficient to keep the locomotive on that trip than to pull it off once it reaches the next railroad. A train operates more efficiently when it keeps running and improves customer service. It is generally billed by horsepower hour which means the railroad pays for the power of a locomotive for the time it is used. For example, if railroad A uses railroad B's 4,000-horsepower locomotive for twelve hours, then railroad A owes railroad B 4,000-horsepower times twelve hours which is 48,000-horsepower hours. Another example is a Union Pacific train with Union Pacific locomotives leaves North Platte, Nebraska, and uses CSX Transportation Railroad to Selkirk,

New York. Those Union Pacific locomotives would normally return west out of Selkirk. There are times when the train reaches its destination, and that locomotive is used for other trips by the receiving railroad before being returned to its home railroad. Hence, this can result in extended stays and the appearance of a locomotive on a route that was not a run through train.

Railroads lease locomotives when a traffic surge requires more locomotives than usual, when more locomotives are out of service for inspection or maintenance than usual, or if a locomotive unexpectedly has to be taken out of service. A hosting railroad will generally handle minor repairs of another railroad's locomotive, because a cost squabble stalling service might be more costly than the repairs. The reason that railroads can easily borrow and lease each other locomotives is that railroad cars and locomotives are designed to work under the Association of American Railroads (ARR) system. Cooperation between railroads improves efficiency and results in faster service.

On March 31, 2018, Union Pacific Locomotive No. 4406 (EMD type SD70M placed in service on June 23, 2001) is a helper with Norfolk Southern Railway locomotive No. 1153 (EMD type SD70ACe placed in service on December 24, 2014) on a northbound Norfolk Southern Railway train at the borough of Taylor, Lackawanna County, Pennsylvania. (*Brian A. Keates photograph*)

Union Pacific locomotive No. 4533 (EMD type SD70M placed in service on December 7, 2001) is a helper on the Pan Am Southern at Ayer, Middlesex County, Massachusetts, in 2014. Pan Am Southern is part of Pan Am Railways which is North America's largest regional railroad system with numerous interchanges such as Canadian Pacific at Mechanicville, New York; CSX at New Haven, Connecticut; Springfield, Massachusetts; and Rotterdam Junction, New York; Norfolk Southern at Mechanicville, New York; Providence & Worcester at Gardner, Massachusetts, and Springfield Terminal at Ayer, Massachusetts. (*Bob Elder photograph*)

In 2014, Union Pacific locomotive No. 5049 (EMD type SD70M placed in service on October 11, 2002) is on the Pan Am Southern at Gardner, Massachusetts. (*Bob Elder photograph*)

On March 31, 2018, a westbound Norfolk Southern Railway general manifest freight train headed by diesel electric locomotive No. 6712 (EMD six-axle 3,800-horsepower type SD60 [originally Conrail No. 6858] built in September 1989) with a Union Pacific Railroad helper locomotive behind it is at the community of Cove in Perry County, Pennsylvania. (*Brian A. Keates photograph*)

Norfolk Southern Railway 4,400 horsepower locomotive No. 7543 (GE type ES44DC placed in service January 5, 2006) with a Norfolk Southern Railway 4,000-horsepower helper No. 8331 (GE type D8-40W built May 1990) and a Union Pacific Railroad helper are leading a westbound tank train through Cove, Pennsylvania, on March 3, 2018. (*Brian A. Keates photograph*)

With a trace of snow on the ground, Norfolk Southern Railway 4,400-horsepower locomotive No. 9409 (GE type D9-44CW placed in service on February 12, 2000) with a Union Pacific Railroad helper locomotive are rolling a northbound general manifest train through Taylor, Pennsylvania, on February 16, 2018. (*Brian A. Keates photograph*)

Under fluffy March 25, 2018 clouds, a westbound empty Norfolk Southern Railway train of coal cars is at Cove, Pennsylvania, headed by Norfolk Southern Railway locomotive No. 9567 (GE type D9-44CW placed in service on December 21, 2000) with trailing Union Pacific Railroad locomotive No. 7440 (GE designation ES44AC, UP designation C45ACCTE built in June 2009). (*Brian A. Keates photograph*)

Southern Railway locomotive No. 9792 (GE type D9-44CW placed in service on March 14, 2003) is heading an eastbound general manifest train with a Union Pacific Railroad helper unit at Cove, Pennsylvania, on March 25, 2019. (*Brian A. Keates photograph*)

On February 20, 2018, Norfolk Southern Railway locomotive No. 9299 (GE type D9-44CW placed in service on May 25, 1999) with Norfolk Southern Railway helper locomotive No. 8090 (GE type ES44AC placed in service March 7, 2011) and a Union Pacific helper locomotive are heading a westbound intermodal train at Cove, Pennsylvania. (*Brian A. Keates photograph*)

A northbound Norfolk Southern Railway intermodal train headed by locomotive No. 9931 (GE type D9-44CW equipped with a cab signal system was placed in service on October 23, 2004) with a Union Pacific Railroad trailing helper unit is at Taylor, Pennsylvania, on April 28, 2018. (*Brian A. Keates photograph*)

Union Pacific Railroad locomotive No. 5514 (GE designation ES44AC, UP designation C45ACCTE placed in service on July 4, 2005) is trailing on a Norfolk Southern Railway general manifest train through Taylor, Pennsylvania, on August 16, 2017. (*Brian A. Keates photograph*)

On November 23, 2018, Union Pacific Railroad locomotive No. 6629 (GE designation AC4400CW; Union Pacific designation C44AC built in May 1997) is leading a Norfolk Southern Railway general manifest train with a Norfolk Southern Railway behind it through Taylor Yard. (*Brian A. Keates photograph*)

Union Pacific Railroad locomotive No. 6963 (6,000-horsepower GE designation AC6000CW originally No. 7574 built in January 2001 repowered and rerated as 4,350-horsepower No. 6963 on August 4, 2010; UP designation C44/60AC) is leading a Norfolk Southern Railway general manifest train through Annville in Lebanon County, Pennsylvania, on August 17, 2017. (*Brian A. Keates photograph*)

In June 2018, Union Pacific Railroad locomotive No. 6787 (GE designation AC4400CW; UP designation C44AC built in May 1996) with two Norfolk Southern Railway locomotives are at Ebensburg Junction, Pennsylvania, running light back to Cresson, Cambria County, Pennsylvania, after handling a loaded corn train. (*D.J. Miller photograph*)

Rear helper units Union Pacific Railroad No. 5074 (EMD type SD70M placed in service on November 9, 2002) with two Norfolk Southern Railway units are pushing at the rear of an R.J. Corman Railroad coal train at Valewood Road in Munster, Cambria County, Pennsylvania, in May 2018. The R.J. Corman Railroad operates a line in central Pennsylvania between the mines and the Norfolk Southern Railway at Cresson, Cambria County, Pennsylvania. (*D.J. Miller photograph*)

After assisting a freight train, a Union Pacific Railroad diesel locomotive along with two Norfolk Southern Railway diesel locomotives are at Ebensburg Junction running light back to Cresson, Pennsylvania, in May 2018. (*D.J. Miller photograph*)

In July 2014, Union Pacific Railroad 4,390-horsepower locomotive No. 5858 (GE designation AC4400CW, UP designation C44ACCTE placed in service on April 24, 2002) is on the rear of a Norfolk Southern Railway power move at Cresson, Pennsylvania. (*D.J. Miller photograph*)

A westbound intermodal train is on the Norfolk Southern Railway mainline at Cresson, Pennsylvania, on November 20, 2021 headed by Norfolk Southern Railway locomotives No. 3662 (GE type ET44AC placed in service March 2, 2017 with ET meaning "Evolution Technology" that is Tier 4 emission compliant), No. 9581 (GE type D9-44CW placed in service on December 30, 2000), and Union Pacific Railroad No. 8151 (GE type ES44AH built in 2014). (*Brian A. Keates photograph*)

This is a close-up view of Union Pacific Railroad No. 8151 in that above November 20, 2021 westbound train scene at Cresson, Pennsylvania. In addition to the large United States flag, the locomotive is lettered "Building America." (*Brian A. Keates photograph*)

On March 10, 2018, helper power on the rear of a westbound coal train at Cove, Pennsylvania, is Norfolk Southern Railway locomotive No. 9928 (GE type D9-44CW placed in service October 22, 2004), Union Pacific Railroad locomotive No. 5865 (GE designation AC4400CW, UP designation C44ACCTE placed in service on January 11, 2003), and another Norfolk Southern Railway locomotive. (*Brian A. Keates photograph*)

An eastbound Norfolk Southern Railway general manifest train is at Cove, Pennsylvania, on March 13, 2019 headed by locomotive No. 9768 (GE type D9-44CW placed in service on February 20, 2003) with trailing Union Pacific Railroad locomotive No. 4519 (EMD type SD70M placed in service December 6, 2001), and another Union Pacific Railroad locomotive. (*Brian A. Keates photograph*)

Union Pacific Railroad locomotives Nos. 1943 (in its special paint scheme honoring the U.S. armed forces originally No. 9026 type SD70AH built by EMD and delivered in August 2016) and 9082 (EMD type SD70AH built in 2017) roll eastbound pulling the Union Pacific Railroad executive train on the Norfolk Southern Railway through Wyomissing, Berks County, Pennsylvania, on May 31, 2018. (*Brian A. Keates photograph*)

From left to right: Union Pacific Railroad locomotive No. 4380 (4,000-horsepower EMD type SD70M placed in service on May 25, 2001) and Canadian National Railway Locomotive No. 8845 (4,000-horsepower EMD type SD70M-2 built in 2007 meeting the EPA's Tier 2 emission regulations) are both trailing on a northbound Norfolk Southern Railway general manifest train at Duncannon, Perry County, Pennsylvania, on March 3, 2018. (*Brian A. Keates photograph*)

At Cove, Perry County, Pennsylvania, Union Pacific Railroad locomotive No. 8903 (EMD type SD70ACe built in 2014 that is designated by Union Pacific as an SD70AH with H for "heavy," because it is ballasted to 428,000 pounds instead of 420,000 pounds) is trailing on a westbound Norfolk Southern Railway intermodal train on August 20, 2018. (*Brian A. Keates photograph*)

On August 26, 2018, Union Pacific Railroad locomotive No. 4460 (EMD type SD70M placed in service on September 5, 2001) is part of a westbound Norfolk Southern Railway general manifest freight train traveling over the Horseshoe Curve (opened on February 15, 1854 by the Pennsylvania Railroad five miles west of the city of Altoona in Blair County, Pennsylvania, to lessen the grade through the Allegheny Mountains). (*Brian A. Keates photograph*)

Union Pacific Railroad locomotive No. 8146 (GE type ES44AH built in 2014) is at the Norfolk Southern Railway Taylor Yard (a freight transfer station where cargo is transferred from trucks to trains and from trains to trucks) in the borough of Taylor, Pennsylvania, on August 11, 2018 with Norfolk Southern Railway locomotive No. 1071 (EMD type SD70ACe painted in the Central Railroad of New Jersey heritage paint scheme at Muncie, Indiana, on June 27, 2012). (*Brian A. Keates photograph*)

On April 20, 2019, Union Pacific Railroad locomotive No. 8038 (GE designation ES44AC, UP designation C45ACCTE built in September 2012) is trailing Norfolk Southern Railway locomotive No. 4272 (originally No. 8956 GE type 9-44CW built March 1996 and rebuilt February 2019 as No. 4272 at the Norfolk Southern Juniata Locomotive Shop with DC to AC lettering and AC waveform under the locomotive cab numbers). This is a Norfolk Southern Railway intermodal train at Sinking Springs, Berks County, Pennsylvania. (*Brian A. Keates photograph*)

On October 23, 2021, Union Pacific Railroad locomotive No. 8864 (EMD type SD70AH built in 2014) is trailing on an eastbound Norfolk Southern Railway general manifest train headed by Norfolk Southern Railway locomotive No. 9580 (GE type D9-44CW placed in service on December 28, 2000) passing by the Altoona, Pennsylvania, Transportation Center. (*Brian A. Keates* photograph)

A Norfolk Southern Railway coal train in May 2018 is passing by the downtown Altoona, Pennsylvania, AMTRAK passenger train station in May 2018 headed by Norfolk Southern Railway locomotive No. 9669 (GE type D9-44CW placed in service on March 8, 2001) and trailing is Union Pacific Railroad No. 4043 (EMD type SD70M placed in service on August 16, 2000). (*D.J. Miller photograph*)

From the previous page, here is a closer look at Union Pacific Railroad locomotive No. 4043 in May 2018 trailing behind lead Norfolk Southern Railway locomotive No. 9669, and trailing behind No. 4043 is Norfolk Southern Railway locomotive No. 9369 (GE type D9-44CW placed in service on May 17, 1999). (*D.J. Miller photograph*)

On November 21, 2021, an eastbound Norfolk Southern Railway train is passing through downtown Altoona, Pennsylvania, with mid train Distributed Power Units Union Pacific Railroad locomotive No. 8029 (GE designation ES44AC, UP designation C45ACCTE built in August 2012) and Norfolk Southern Railway locomotive No. 1073 (EMD type SD70ACe in the Penn Central Railroad heritage paint scheme completed at Muncie, Indiana, on June 27, 2012 and placed in service that date). (*D.J. Miller photograph*)

Union Pacific Railroad locomotive No. 2517 (3,800-horsepower type SD60M originally No. 6356 built in October 1992) is assisting a Norfolk Southern Railway train passing through Altoona, Pennsylvania, in April 2018. (*D.J. Miller photograph*)

On August 2018, Norfolk Southern Railway locomotive No. 9872 (GE type D9-44CW placed in service on May 7, 2004) is departing Altoona, Pennsylvania, with two Union Pacific locomotives behind it to help handle the oil train. (*D.J. Miller photograph*)

On August 9, 2019, Kansas City Southern locomotive No. 4802 GE type ES44AC (one of 20 Nos. 4790-4809 of this type built in 2012) is on Union Pacific Railroad trackage at Topeka, Kansas, helping to pull the freight train north across the Kansas River. (*Brian A. Keates photograph*)

Kansas City Southern locomotive No. 4116 EMD type SD70ACe (one of seventeen of this type Nos. 4100–4116 built during February–March 2008) is pulling a general manifest local train into the Union Pacific Railroad Topeka yard on September 1, 2021. (*Brian A. Keates photograph*)

Norfolk Southern Railway locomotive No. 2599 (4,000-horsepower EMD type SD70M placed in service on May 13, 2003) and Union Pacific No. 8781 (EMD type SD70ACe delivered on June 28, 2012) are trailing on a westbound general manifest train pulling through Topeka, Kansas. (*Brian A. Keates photograph*)

On October 19, 2019, Norfolk Southern Railway locomotive No. 9403 (GE type D9-44CW placed in service on February 6, 2000) is moving around the Union Pacific Railroad Topeka, Kansas, yard. (*Brian A. Keates photograph*)

A Progress Rail locomotive is trailing on a Union Pacific Railroad general manifest train over the Union Pacific Railroad high line in Kansas City, Missouri, on August 31, 2021. Progress Rail has been a provider of diesel electric locomotive technology handling EMD freight, passenger, repowered, and used locomotives. (*Brian A. Keates photograph*)

Union Pacific Railroad locomotive No. 7263 (GE designation AC4400CW; UP designation C44AC built in November 1999) is trailing on a Norfolk Southern Railway eastbound coal train at Cove, Pennsylvania, on July 19, 2019. (*Brian A. Keates photograph*)

7

Tunnel Inn Greets Union Pacific at Gallitzin

The Tunnel Inn at 702 Jackson Street in Gallitzin, Pennsylvania (telephone Number 814-408-2186), is located overlooking the western portal of the double track 3,612-foot-long Allegheny Tunnel completed in 1854 (now used by Norfolk Southern Railway trains) and the parallel abandoned 3,612-foot-long Gallitzin Tunnel completed in 1904. In 1995, the Allegheny Tunnel was enlarged for double-stack container traffic and widened to allow two tracks with each track handling eastbound and westbound trains. The Gallitzin Tunnel was taken out of service, and tracks were removed in 1995.

The two-story brick Tunnel Inn was built in 1905 as the Gallitzin Fire House with a tall bell tower at the rear of the building. Next the building housed the Borough of Gallitzin offices, a library on the second floor, and the Gallitzin Police Department with a garage bay for a patrol car, and holding cells in the basement. In the late 1980s, a new town office, library, and police station were built on the north side of the tracks. A private individual and his wife purchased the building in the early 1990s. They carefully and extensively remodeled the building creating the Tunnel Inn. This was a trackside bed and breakfast with four rental suites that catered to railroad hobbyists and students of rail transportation. In 2013, the private individual and his wife retired, closed the inn to the public, and used the inn as a private family vacation home.

In April 2008, Bob Elder, a lifelong rail fan who had traveled to numerous railroad hot spots from Maine to Florida, visited the Tunnel Inn and was amazed that in all of this travels nothing compared with the Tunnel Inn. It became a dream that came true and with a lot of hard work made it possible for Elder to have a career as the innkeeper of The Tunnel Inn.

On June 12, 2018, Union Pacific Railroad locomotive No. 1943 (with its special paint scheme that signifies Union Pacific's long relationship with the U.S. armed forces) is leading a westbound Norfolk Southern Railway (NS) freight train passing by the north side of the Tunnel Inn property in Gallitzin, Pennsylvania. Former Pennsylvania Railroad caboose No. 477852, shown on the upper left of the picture at the Tunnels Park and Museum, is north of the NS two track main line that uses the Allegheny Tunnel. The gravel path behind the locomotive once had trackage that used the Gallitzin Tunnel until it was closed in 1995. (*Bob Elder photograph*)

A westbound Norfolk Southern Railway intermodal train has emerged from the Allegheny Tunnel as seen from the lawn of the Tunnel Inn at Gallitzin, Pennsylvania, on July 8, 2021 with Union Pacific Railroad helper locomotive No. 7754 (GE designation ES44AC, UP designation C45ACCTE built in August 2007). (*Bob Elder photograph*)

On November 20, 2021, a westbound Norfolk Southern Railway general manifest train has exited the Allegheny Tunnel at Gallitzin, Pennsylvania, headed by Norfolk Southern Railway locomotive No. 9780 (GE type D9-44CW placed in service on February 28, 2003) and Union Pacific Railroad helper locomotive No. 8224 (GE type ES44AH built in 2014). (*Bob Elder photograph*)

On November 14, 2021, a five-unit westbound Norfolk Southern Railway general manifest train is passing under the Jackson Street bridge that is used by rail enthusiasts to view and photograph trains and by local residents as a path through Gallitzin, Pennsylvania. The third locomotive is Union Pacific Railroad No. 3060 (EMD type SD70ACe-T4 one of forty-eight (Nos. 3014–3061) built during 2016–2017), and the fourth unit is Norfolk Southern Railway No. 7690 (GE type ES44DC placed in service on December 20, 2007). (*Bob Elder photograph*)

On November 21, 2021, an eastbound Norfolk Southern Railway train is passing through the Allegheny Tunnel in Gallitzin, Pennsylvania, with middle of the train Distributed Power Units Union Pacific Railroad locomotive No. 8029 (GE designation ES44AC, UP designation C45ACCTE built in August 2012) and Norfolk Southern Railway locomotive No. 1073 (EMD type SD70ACe placed in service and painting completed in the Penn Central Railroad heritage paint scheme at Muncie, Indiana on June 27, 2012). This same train was later photographed at Altoona shown on bottom picture on page 104. (*D.J. Miller photograph*)

In July 2014, a Norfolk Southern Railway locomotive No. 9625 (GE type D9-44CW placed in service on February 8, 2001) with trailing Union Pacific locomotive No. 2002 (originally built in August 2001 as No. 4691 EMD type SD70M) specially painted to honor the 2002 Olympic Winter Games, and trailing behind it another Norfolk Southern Railway locomotive has just past under the Main Street bridge in Gallitzin, Pennsylvania. This eastbound train shortly used the single track 1,600-foot-long New Portage Tunnel which is about a half-mile south of the Gallitzin Tunnel. Just south of this track is Portage Street which connects Main Street with Tunnelhill Street in Gallitzin. (*D.J. Miller photograph*)

This is a close up of Union Pacific locomotive No. 2002 in July 2014 shown in the above view east of the Main Street bridge in Gallitzin, Pennsylvania. The 2002 Salt Lake City Olympic Flame was carried by a special Union Pacific train powered by custom painted locomotives Nos. 2001 and 2002. That was the second time the Olympic Flame moved by rail in the United States. Union Pacific transported the Olympic for the Atlanta 1996 Centennial Olympic Games. (*D.J. Miller photograph*)

An eastbound Norfolk Southern Railway freight train is passing by the side yard of the Tunnel Inn with Union Pacific Railroad locomotive No. 8828 (EMD type SD70AH built in 2014) under the Jackson Street bridge in Gallitzin, Pennsylvania, on September 15, 2020. The sign "Thank You Railroaders" in the bottom of the photograph was hand painted by the co-author of this book Beth Anne Keates. (*Bob Elder photograph*)

Westbound Norfolk Southern Railway locomotive No. 3401 (EMD 3,000-horsepower type SD40-2 originally Conrail No. 6475 built in November1978) with two Union Pacific helper locomotives have emerged from the Allegheny Tunnel and have just past under the Jackson Street bridge in Gallitzin, Pennsylvania, in July 2014. Introduced in January 1972, the reliability and versatility of the SD40-2 locomotive ranked it second in sales (GP9 was first). The SD40-2 with its modular electronic control systems was an improvement over the SD40. (*D.J. Miller photograph*)

Taken from the deck of the Tunnel Inn on the snow covered day of January 25, 2018, in the middle of a westbound Norfolk Southern Railway train; Union Pacific Railroad locomotive No. 4012 (Distributed Power Unit EMD type SD70M placed in service July14, 2000) is going under the Jackson Street bridge in Gallitzin, Pennsylvania. This locomotive has the same number as Union Pacific Railroad No. 4012 Big Boy on display at Steamtown in Scranton, Pennsylvania. (*Bob Elder photographer*)

In this January 25, 2018 scene on the other side of the bridge with the Tunnel Inn (brick building with elevated back roofed porch) and view of snow-covered Gallitzin, Pennsylvania, Norfolk Southern Railway helper locomotives No. 6318 (originally Conrail No. 6707 built in November 1983 and was rebuilt and became No. 6318 type SD40E in October 13, 2009) and No. 9822 (GE type D9-44CW placed in service on March 17, 2004) plus a Union Pacific Railroad locomotive are passing under the Jackson Street bridge. (*Bob Elder photographer*)

On January 25, 2018, with former Pennsylvania Railroad caboose No. 477852 in the upper left of the picture at the Tunnels Park and Museum, a westbound Norfolk Southern Railway intermodal freight is passing by the snow-covered grounds of the Tunnel Inn with Union Pacific Railroad locomotive helper unit No. 3970 (EMD type SD70M placed in service on September 27, 2003) soon to go under the Jackson Street bridge in Gallitzin, Pennsylvania. (*Bob Elder photographer*)

In August 2014, Norfolk Southern Railway locomotive No. 1119 (EMD type SD70ACe placed in service on March 29, 2014) is heading five locomotives of which three are Union Pacific Railroad locomotives on a westbound intermodal train emerging from the Allegheny tunnel and passing under the Jackson Street bridge in Gallitzin, Pennsylvania. (*D.J. Miller photograph*)

Norfolk Southern Railway locomotive No. 7569 (GE type ES44DC placed in service on June 16, 2006) and Union Pacific Railroad helper locomotive No. 4585 (EMD type SD70M placed in service on March 26, 2001) are passing just east of the Jackson Street bridge by the side of the cliff where the Tunnel Inn is located in Gallitzin, Pennsylvania, in August 2014. (*D.J. Miller photograph*)

On the evening of April 30, 2021, a Norfolk Southern Railway westbound intermodal train is passing by the Tunnel Inn at Gallitzin, Pennsylvania, with the floodlights illuminating Union Pacific Railroad locomotive No. 8993 (EMD type SD70AH built in December 2014). Note the rail hobbyist by the guard rail is in a wonderful position to get the perfect photo. (*Bob Elder photograph*)

8

Union Pacific Passenger Service

Union Pacific Railroad began its passenger service in July 1866. In the beginning, passenger trains seldom exceeded 20 miles per hour. Train passengers ate their meals in station dining halls. George Mortimer Pullman (March 3, 1831–October 19, 1897) developed a railroad sleeping car in 1864. Pullman introduced his first "hotel on wheels" in 1867 which was a sleeper car equipped with an attached kitchen and dining car. Passenger train service from Omaha to San Francisco began five days after the golden spike was driven on May 10, 1869. On December 5, 1888, the Southern Pacific Company joined with the Union Pacific Railroad to introduce the "Golden Gate Special" between San Francisco/Oakland via Ogden to Council Bluffs where passengers transferred to the Chicago & Northwestern Railroad. Passenger revenues peaked in 1921; however, as automobile ownership increased, railroad passenger ridership declined. In February 1934, Union Pacific introduced M10000, a lightweight streamlined articulated (all cars were permanently coupled) passenger train built by Pullman Standard with components from Winton (General Motors) and General Electric and went on a publicity tour around the United States. It was placed in daily service in 1936 as the City of Salina connecting Kansas City with Salina, Kansas, and was scrapped in 1942 to contribute aluminum to the war effort. According to the Union Pacific website, "over the next couple of decades, Union Pacific made substantial additions to their passenger service equipment. Between 1946 and 1965, new purchases included 291 sleeping cars, 196 coaches, 112 diners and lounges, sixteen dome coaches, and eleven dome diners (unique to UP)." Some of Union Pacific passenger trains were as follows:

The *City of San Francisco* was a streamlined through passenger train that operated from June 14, 1936 to 1971 via the Overland Route between Chicago, Illinois and Oakland, California with a bus connection train side at Oakland (16th Street) to San Francisco (3rd & Townsend Station) via the Bay Bridge and had a running time of thirty-nine hours and forty-five minutes each way. This was a Pullman-built eleven-car articulated streamline train with two diesel electric power unit cars, a baggage mail car, a baggage-dormitory-kitchen car, a diner-lounge car, four sleeper cars, a forty-eight-scat chair car, and a thirty-eight-seat coach-buffet-blind end observation car. It was owned and operated jointly by the Chicago & Northwestern Railway (1936–1955), Chicago,

Milwaukee, St. Paul and Pacific Railroad (1955–1971), Union Pacific Railroad, and Southern Pacific Company. On October 30, 1955, the Milwaukee Road replaced the Chicago & North Western between Chicago and Omaha. In 1960, the *City of San Francisco* was combined with the *City of Los Angeles* east of Ogden.

The *City of Los Angeles* was a streamlined passenger train operating from May 15, 1936 to May 1, 1971 between Chicago, Illinois and Los Angeles, California via Omaha, Nebraska and Ogden, Utah. Between Chicago and Omaha, it ran on the Chicago & North Western Railway until October 1955 and thereafter on the Milwaukee Road. The *City of Los Angeles* was combined with the *City of San Francisco* in 1960, and was terminated when Amtrak took over Union Pacific's rail passenger service on May 1, 1971.

The *City of Portland* operated from June 1935 to May 1, 1971 between Chicago, Illinois and Portland, Oregon. It used Chicago & Northwestern Railway between Chicago and Omaha until 1955 and thereafter the Milwaukee Road. It was terminated when Amtrak took over Union Pacific's rail passenger service on May 1, 1971.

The *City of Denver* operated June 18, 1936 to May 1, 1971 between Chicago, Illinois, and Denver, Colorado. From 1936 to 1955, it used Chicago & Northwestern Railway between Chicago and Omaha and thereafter the Milwaukee Road. It was terminated by Amtrak on May 1, 1971, because Amtrak preferred Burlington's Chicago to Denver route.

The *City of St. Louis* operated from June 2, 1946 to May 1, 1971 between St. Louis, Missouri, and Cheyenne, Wyoming. In April 1951, it became a separate train from St. Louis to Los Angeles, California. It was combined with the *City of Los Angeles* west of Ogden, Utah, in 1964, and in 1968 with the *City of San Francisco* from Cheyenne to Ogden. Between St. Louis and Kansas City, the train operated on the Wabash Railroad. It later became the *City of Kansas City* which was terminated when Amtrak took over on May 1, 1971.

On May 1, 1971, under the Railroad Passenger Service Act, Amtrak took over intercity passenger train service in the United States. Amtrak operates over several routes on UP. On June 23, 1995, Union Pacific Railroad acquired the Chicago & Northwestern which included C&NW's Chicago's metropolitan commuter rail services: Metra's UP/North, UP/Northwest, and UP/West Lines, all of which operate from the Ogilvie Transportation Center (the former North Western Station).

215

UNION PACIFIC RAILROAD.

COMPLETED, AND IN CONNECTION WITH THE CENTRAL PACIFIC RAILROAD,

FORMS THE SHORTEST ROUTE TO

SACRAMENTO, SAN FRANCISCO, CHINA AND JAPAN.

OLIVER AMES, President, Boston, Mass.
J. DUFF, Vice-President, "
J. M. S. WILLIAMS, Treasurer, "
E. H. ROLLINS, Secretary, "
C. G. HAMMOND, Gen. Supt., Omaha, Neb.
C. W. MEAD, Asst. Gen. Supt., "

J. R. NICHOLS, Asst. Supt., Omaha, Neb.
FRANCIS COLTON, Gen. Pass'r Agent, "
H. BROWNSON, Gen. Freight Agent, "
S. H. H. CLARK, Supt. Platte Division, "
C. H. CHAPPELL, Supt. Lodge Pole Division, Cheyenne, W. T.

L. FILLMORE, Supt. Laramie Division, Laramie, W. T.
E. W. WEED, Supt. Utah Div., Wasatch, Utah.
GEO. STARR, Gen. Traveling Agt, Chicago, Ill.
FERD. KNOWLAND, Gen. Eastern Agent, 303 Broadway, N. Y.

PLATTE DIVISION.—S. H. H. CLARK, Div. Supt., May 16, 1870.

Going West Mixed.	Going West Express.	Mls	STATIONS.	Going East Frs.	Going East Express.	Going East Mixed.
			LEAVE] [ARRIVE			
6 00 P.M.	10 30 A.M.	0	......Omaha[1]......		3 45 P.M.	7 45 P.M.
6 20 "	....	4	...Summit Siding...		.... "	7 20 "
6 50 "	11 25 "	10	......Gilmore......		2 35 "	6 50 "
7 15 "	12 40 A.M.	12	......Papillion......		2 20 "	6 20 "
8 30 "	12 15 P.M.	29	......Elkhorn......		1 45 "	4 50 "
9 05 "	12 35 "	35	......Valley......		1 25 "	4 00 "
10 00 "	1 20 "	47	......Fremont......		1 00 "	3 00 "
11 15 P.M.	2 00 "	62	....North Bend....		12 00 N'N.	12 40 P.M.
12 25 A.M.	2 35 "	76	......Schuyler......		11 25 A.M.	11 25 A.M.
1 40 "	3 15 "	92	......Columbus......		10 40 A.M.	10 10 "
2 15 "	....	99	......Jackson......		....	9 30 "
3 05 "	4 00 "	109	....Silver Creek....		9 50 "	8 40 "
4 00 "	....	121	......Clark's......		....	7 45 "
5 00 "	4 55 "	132	.....Lone Tree.....		8 50 "	6 50 "
6 00 "	....	142	.....Chapman's		....	6 00 "
7 00 "	5 50 "	154	arr } Grand { lve		7 50 "	5 10 "
7 50 "	6 10 "	154	lve } Island { arr		7 30 "	4 30 "
8 30 "	....	162	......Pawnee......		....	3 50 "
9 20 "	6 58 "	172	....Wood River....		6 50 "	2 55 "
10 10 "	....	183	......Gibbon......		....	2 00 "
10 55 "	7 48 "	191	......Kearney......		6 05 "	1 20 "
11 40 A.M.	8 10 "	201	.....Stevenson.....		....	12 35 A.M.
12 30 P.M.	8 35 "	212	.....Elm Creek.....		5 15 "	11 40 P.M.
1 15 "	....	221	......Overton......		4 53	10 50 "
2 00 "	9 25 "	230	....Plum Creek....		4 30 "	10 00 "
2 55 "	....	240	......Cayote......		4 05	8 40 "
3 40 "	10 15 "	250	...Willow Island...		3 42 "	7 55 "
4 30 "	....	260	......Warren......		....	7 05 "
5 05 "	11 00 "	268	...Brady Island....		2 58 "	6 30 "
5 50 "	12 25 P.M.	278	...McPherson....		2 35 "	5 50 "
7 00 P.M.	12 00 N'T.	291	...North Platte...		2 00 A.M.	4 45 P.M.
			ARRIVE] [LEAVE			

LARAMIE DIVISION. L. FILMORE, Div. Supt.

Going West Mixed.	Going West Express.	Mls	STATIONS.	Going East Frs.	Going East Express.	Going East Mixed.
			LEAVE] [ARRIVE			
10 00 P.M.	1 40 P.M.	573	......Laramie......		9 20 A.M.	2 45 P.M.
11 20 P.M.	2 30 "	588	......Wyoming......		8 40 "	1 20 "
12 20 A.M.	3 00 "	603	...Cooper's Lake...		8 15 "	12 30 P.M.
1 10 "	3 25 "	607	......Lookout......		7 50 "	11 45 A.M.
1 45 "	3 50 "	616	......Miser......		7 25 "	10 55 "
2 20 "	4 15 "	624	....Rock Creek....		7 00 "	10 10 "
3 45 "	5 00 "	640	......Como......		6 20 "	8 50 "
4 20 "	5 20 "	647	...Medicine Bow...		5 55 "	8 05 "
5 30 "	5 50 "	656	......Carbon......		5 30 "	7 20 "
6 00 "	6 05 "	664	......Simpson......		5 15 "	6 55 "
6 30 "	6 20 "	669	......Percy......		4 55 "	6 30 "
7 00 "	6 35 "	675	......Dana......		4 40 "	5 50 "
7 30 "	6 55 "	682	...St. Mary's...		4 20 "	5 00 "
8 25 "	7 30 "	697	.. Fort Steele.....		3 45 "	3 45 "
9 05 "	7 55 "	704	......Grenville......		3 20 "	3 00 "
9 40 "	8 20 "	711	arr } Rawlins { lve		3 00 "	2 20 "
10 00 "	8 50 "	711	lve } { arr		2 40 "	1 50 "
11 15 A.M.	9 30 "	724	.....Separation.....		1 55 "	12 40 A.M.
12 35 P.M.	10 20 "	739	......Creston......		1 05 "	11 25 P.M.
1 40 "	11 00 "	754	....Wash-a-kie....		12 05 A.M.	10 00 "
2 20 "	11 35 P.M.	763	....Red Desert....		11 35 P.M.	9 10 "
3 30 "	12 35 A.M.	776	....Table Rock....		10 55 "	8 00 "
4 20 "	12 45 "	786	arr } Bitter { lve		10 20 "	7 00 "
4 30 "	1 00 "	786	lve } Creek { arr		10 00 "	6 30 "
5 10 "	1 28 "	795	....Black Buttes....		9 32 "	5 45 "
5 25 "	1 40 "	799	......Hallville......		9 20 "	5 25 "
6 00 "	2 03 "	807	...Point of Rocks...		9 00 "	4 50 "
6 50 "	2 40 "	818	......Salt Wells....		8 30 "	3 50 "
7 50 "	3 25 "	832	...Rock Springs...		7 50 "	2 45 "
9 00 "	4 10 "	847	...Green River....		7 10 "	1 40 "
10 20 P.M.	5 00 A.M.	860	......Bryan[3]......		6 30 P.M.	12 30 P.M.
			ARRIVE] [LEAVE			

LODGE POLE DIVISION.

C. H. CHAPPEL, Div. Superintendent, Cheyenne, W. T.

Going West Mixed.	Going West Express.	Mls	STATIONS.	Going East Frs.	Going East Express.	Going East Mixed.
			LEAVE] [ARRIVE			
7 30 P.M.	12 20 A.M.	291	...North Platte...		1 40 A.M.	4 10 P.M.
8 15 "	....	295	......Nichols......		....	3 30 "
8 50 "	1 00 "	299	...O'Fallon's		1 00 "	2 55 "
10 00 "	1 30 "	322	......Alkali......		12 20 A.M.	1 50 "
10 40 "	....	332	......Roscoe......		....	1 05 "
11 30 P.M.	2 15 "	342	......Ogalalla......		11 30 P.M.	12 20 P.M.
12 20 A.M.	....	351	......Brule......		....	11 35 A.M.
1 15 "	3 00 "	361	....Big Spring.....		10 35 P.M.	10 50 "
2 40 "	3 35 "	377	.....Julesburg.....		9 55 "	9 35 "
4 20 "	4 20 "	397	....Lodge Pole....		9 03 "	8 10 "
5 45 "	5 00 "	414	arr } Sidney { lve		8 20 "	6 50 "
6 20 "	5 15 "	414	lve } { arr		8 00 "	6 20 "
8 00 "	6 00 "	443	......Potter......		7 05 "	4 45 "
9 40 "	6 43 "	451	.....Antelope.....		6 15 "	3 20 "
10 40 "	....	463	......Bushnell......		....	2 20 "
11 30 A.M.	7 35 "	473	.....Pine Bluff.....		5 15 "	1 35 "
12 30 P.M.	....	484	......Egbert......		....	12 40 A.M.
1 30 "	8 31 "	496	......Hillsdale......		4 15 "	11 40 P.M.
2 35 "	....	508	......Archer......		....	10 40 "
3 20 "	9 20 A.M.	516	arr } Cheyenne { lve		3 20 "	10 00 "
4 30 "	10 00 "		lve } { arr		2 30 "	9 30 "
5 10 "	10 12 "	522	......Hazard......		2 00 "	9 00 "
5 55 "	10 55 "	531	......Otto......		....	8 15 "
6 30 "	11 15 "	536	.. Granite Canon ..		1 10 "	7 45 "
7 10 "	....	543	......Buford......		....	7 10 "
7 50 "	12 10 P.M.	549	......Sherman......		12 10 P.M.	6 30 "
8 35 "	....	557	......Harney......		11 30 A.M.	5 35 "
9 10 "	1 05 "	564	....Red Buttes....		11 05 "	5 00 "
9 45 "	1 30 "	570	...Fort Sanders....		10 40 "	4 20 "
10 00 P.M.	1 40 P.M.	573	......Laramie......		10 30 A.M.	4 00 P.M.
			ARRIVE] [LEAVE			

UTAH DIVISION.—E. W. WEED, Div. Supt.

Mixed.	Express.	Mls	STATIONS.	Frs.	Express.	Mixed.
11 00 P.M.	5 50 A.M.	860	......Bryan......		6 00 P.M.	12 00 N'N.
12 20 A.M.	6 50 "	877	......Granger......		5 18 "	10 40 A.M.
1 10 "	7 30 "	889	...Church Buttes...		4 50 "	9 50 "
2 30 "	8 30 "	906	......Carter......		4 05 "	8 30 "
3 20 "	9 05 "	915	......Bridger......		3 40 "	7 45 "
4 40 "	10 00 "	930	......Piedmont......		2 55 "	6 30 "
5 40 "	10 50 "	939	......Aspen......		2 15 "	5 40 "
7 15 "	11 55 A.M.	957	.....Evanston.....		1 15 "	4 00 "
8 15 "	12 40 P.M.	968	arr } Wasatch { lve		12 40 "	3 00 "
8 35 "	1 10 "	968	lve } { arr		12 10 P.M.	2 15 "
9 15 "	1 40 "	976	....Castle Rock....		11 25 A.M.	1 10 A.M.
10 30 A.M.	2 40 "	993	......Echo......		10 30 "	11 40 P.M.
11 50 "	3 30 "	1009	......Weber		9 30 "	10 15 "
12 50 P.M.	4 10 "	1021	....Devil's Gate....		8 50 "	9 10 "
1 20 "	4 25 "	1024	....Uintah[4]		8 25 "	8 40 "
2 00 P.M.	5 00 P.M.	1032	......Ogden[5]......		8 00 A.M.	8 00 P.M.
			ARRIVE] [LEAVE			

Hotel Express train bound West leaves Omaha Tuesdays and Thursdays, as second (2) section of regular express leaving Omaha 10 30 a.m.

Hotel Express train bound East leaves Ogden Wednesday and Saturday, as second (2) section of express train leaving Ogden 8 00 a.m.

STANDARD OF TIME.—Trains are run by Omaha time from Omaha to Laramie, (Omaha time being one hour and twenty-eight minutes slower than New York time. From Laramie to Ogden trains are run by Laramie time, which is two hours shorter than New York time).

DIRECT CONNECTIONS MADE

1 At Omaha with Chicago and Northwestern; Chicago, Rock Island and Pacific, Burlington and Missouri River, and St. Joseph and Council Bluffs Railroads; also with Missouri River Line of Packets to and from all principal Eastern and Southern cities.

2 At Cheyenne with Denver Pacific Railroad for Denver, Golden City, Central City, Santa Fe and all points in Colorado and New Mexico.

3 At Bryan with stages for the Great Sweetwater Mining District.

4 At Ogden with Utah Central Railroad for Salt Lake City and Southern Utah.

5 At Ogden with Central Pacific Railway for White Pine Silver Mines, Sacramento, San Francisco and principal cities in California, Nevada and Idaho.

The May 16, 1870 Union Pacific Railroad schedule from the *June 1870 Travelers Official Guide of the Railways and Steam Navigation Lines in the United States & Canada* shows the passenger service from Omaha via North Platte, Laramie, and Bryan to Ogden. Between Omaha and Ogden, the mixed train made almost 100 stops while the express train made about eighty stops.

789

UNION PACIFIC SYSTEM

New and Direct Route to Yellowstone National Park

UNION PACIFIC RAILROAD CO.

For List of System Officers, see page 778.

GENERAL OFFICES.

Fifteenth and Dodge Streets, Omaha, Neb.

A. L. MOHLER, President, Omaha, Neb.

J. A. MUNROE, Vice-President, Omaha, Neb. | N. H. LOOMIS, General Solicitor, Omaha, Neb.
| T. M. ORR, Assistant to President, »

TRAFFIC DEPARTMENT.

J. A. MUNROE, Vice-President, Omaha, Neb.

C. J. LANE, General Freight Agent, Omaha, Neb. | W. S. BASINGER, General Passenger Agent, Omaha. Neb.
W. H. GARRATT, Asst. General Freight Agent, » | W. H. MURRAY, Asst. General Passenger Agent, »
G. W. HAMILTON, Asst. General Freight Agent, » | R. S. RUBLE, Asst. General Passenger Agent. Denver, Colo.
C. W. AXTELL, Asst. General Freight Agent, » | W. K. CUNDIFF, Asst. General Passenger Agent. Kansas City, Mo.
H. G. KAILL, Gen. Freight and Passenger Agt., Kansas City, Mo. | GEO. L. ALLEY, General Baggage Agent, Omaha, Neb.
F. B. CHOATE, Assistant General Freight Agent, Denver, Colo. | R. A. SMITH, Colonization and Industrial Agent, »
W. H. HANCOCK, Freight Claim Agent, Omaha, Neb.

MAINTENANCE AND OPERATING DEPARTMENTS.

CHARLES WARE, General Manager, Omaha, Neb. | W. M. JEFFERS, General Superintendent, Omaha, Neb.
C. E. FULLER, Supt. Motive Power and Machinery, » | E. L. FRIES, General Storekeeper, »
R. L. HUNTLEY, Chief Engineer, » | A. B. RUTHERFORD, Stationer, »
W. D. LINCOLN, Superintendent Transportation, » | SAMUEL J. PETERSON, General Claims Agent, »
G. O. BROPHY, Superintendent Nebraska Division, » | P. F. FRENZER, Superintendent of Telegraph, »
S. R. TOUCEY, Supt. Wyoming Division, Cheyenne, Wyo. | F. E. LEWIS, Manager Dining Cars and Hotels, »
A. F. VICK ROY, Supt. Colorado Division, Denver, Colo. | E. C. SUTTON, Supt. Dining Cars and Hotels, »
R. L. DAVIS, Supt. Kansas Division, Kansas City, Mo. | AUGUST F. JONAS, M.D., Chief Surgeon, »
GEO. C. SMITH, Purchasing Agent, Omaha, Neb. | ARTHUR W. SCRIBNER, Tax Commissioner, »
| W. R. McKEEN, Jr., Consulting Engineer of Motor Cars, »

LAW DEPARTMENT.

N. H. LOOMIS, General Solicitor, Omaha, Neb.

EDSON RICH, Assistant General Solicitor, Omaha, Neb. | J. W. LACEY, General Attorney for Wyoming, Cheyenne, Wyo.
R. W. BLAIR, Gen. Att'y for Kansas and Missouri, Topeka, Kan. | P. L. WILLIAMS, General Attorney for Utah, Salt Lake, Utah.
CLAYTON C. DORSEY, Gen. Attorney for Colorado, Denver, Colo.

TREASURY AND ACCOUNTING DEPARTMENTS.

H. J. STIRLING, Auditor, Omaha, Neb. | F. W. CHARSKE, Auditor of Freight Accounts, Omaha, Neb.
W. B. WILKINS, Assistant Auditor, » | B. LANCASTER, Auditor of Disbursements, »
F. B. SOUTHARD, Auditor of Passenger Accounts, » | M. L. STONE, Aud. of Equipment Service Accounts, »
W. H. SANFORD, Assistant Treasurer, Omaha, Neb.

MISCELLANEOUS.

J. A. GRIFFITH, Land Commissioner U. P. R.R. Co. and General Manager The U. P. Land Co., Omaha, Neb.

American Express Company.

MAIN LINE—OMAHA TO OGDEN.

Westbound (read down). Train numbers and names across the top; the columns Los Ang. Lim. 7 and Overland Lim 1 carry the vertical legend "See Special Notice on page 782" across the local-stop rows, and St'msburg Local •27 carries "Via Beatrice and Stromsburg Branch." across its mid-line rows.

Grand Isl. Local. •23	St'msburg Local. •27	North Platte Local. •25	Denver Spl. 11	Pacific Lim. 19	Colorado Spl. 13	Colorado Exp. 15	California Mail. 3	Los Ang. Lim. 7	Ore.-Wash Lim. 17	Overland Lim 1	Miles	Table 1. June, 1916.
11 20	9 35	6 05	6 05	.....	10 45	11 20	11 20	10 00	9 35	7 00	o	LEAVE] Chicago (C. & N. W.) [ARRIVE
3 30	10 15	7 20	7 20	.....	12 10	3 30	3 30	11 40	10 15	7 30	491	arr..Omaha » lve
10 30	6 05	6 05	6 05	10 45	10 45	10 30	10 30	.....	.....	.....	o	(C. M. & St. P.) lve...Chicago....arr
3 25	7 35	7 35	7 35	12 15	12 15	3 25	3 25	.....	.....	.....	492	arr....Omaha....lve
*4 55	†12 01	*7 35	*7 05	*12 01 Night	*11 20	*3 21	*3 25	*11 25	*10 00	*7 15		(Central time.) lv.Council Bluffs.ar
5 05	12 16	7 50	7 20	12 15	11 35	3 56	3 40	11 40	10 15	7 30		arr....Omaha....lve
*5 30	†12 41	*8 15	*7 45	*12 40	*12 30	*4 20	*4 30	*11 55	*10 30	*8 00	o	lve..+Omaha ♂..arr
5 40	12 54	8 30	—	.....	.....	.....	.....	See Spl. Notice p.782	.....	See Spl. Notice p.782	4	...South Omaha...
5 51	1 05	8 40	—	.....	.....	.....	.....		.....		10	....Gilmore.....
6 02	1 15	8 51	—	.....	.....	.....	.....		.....		15	....Papillion.....
6 15	1 26	9 03	—	.....	.....	.....	.....		.....		20	.....Millard.....
6 32	1 42	9 20	—	—	—	n -	—		—		29	.....Elkhorn......
6 38	1 50	9 27	—	—	—	n -	—		—		31	...Waterloo......
6 47	2 00	9 36	—	—	—	n -	5 18		z -		35	.....Valley..
7 08	Via Beatrice and Stromsburg Branch.	10 05	8 42	1 40	1 27	5 26	5 40	12 50	11 33	8 53	46	+....Fremont.....
7 22		10 16	—	—	—	n -	—		—		53	.....Ames........
7 38		10 31	—	—	—	n -	—		—		61	+...North Bend....
7 53		10 45	—	—	—	n -	—		—		68	+.....Rogers .....
8 08		10 59	9 19	2 18	v -	n -	6 23		12 12		76	+....Schuyler .....
8 21		11 15	—	—	—	n -	—		—		84	+....Richland ....
8 39		12 05	9 42	2 43	2 25	6 57	6 56	1 47	12 36	9 51	91	+....Columbus ....
8 55		12 20	—	—	—	n -	—		—		99	....Duncan......
9 15		12 40	—	—	—	n -	—		—		109	....Silver Creek....
9 26		12 52	—	—	—	n -	—		—		115	.....Havens ....
9 37		1 03	—	—	—	n -	—		—		121	.....Clarks....
9 48		1 13	—	—	—	n -	—		—		126	.....Thummel......
9 59	7 10	1 25	10 36	3 44	—	7 42	8 05	1 56	—	—	132	+...Central City..
—		1 31	—	—	—	n -	—		—		135	.....Paddock......
10 16	7 27	1 40	—	—	—	n -	—		—		142	......Chapman ....
10 40	7 50	2 00	11 05	4 20	3 49	8 20	8 45	3 15	2 10	11 20	154	ar.+ Grand Island .lv.
PM	PM	2 25	11 10	4 25	3 54	8 25	8 50	3 20	2 15	11 25	154	lv. Grand Island ♂ ar.
.....	.....	2 40	—	—	—	n -	9 05		—		161	.....Alda ....
.....	.....	2 54	—	4 53	—	n -	9 20		—		169	....Wood River.....
.....	.....	3 07	—	5 07	—	n -	9 35		—		177	.....Shelton ......
.....	.....	3 17	—	5 20	—	n -	9 48		—		183	......Gibbon......
.....	.....	3 32	—	—	—	n -	—		—		191	.....Buda ......
.....	.....	3 55	12 10	5 45	4 51	8 54	10 19	4 19	3 15	12 21	196	+....Kearney .... [ARRIVE]
	P M	A M	A M	A M	A M	P M	P M	P M	P M	P M	P M	LEAVE]

Eastbound (read up). The columns Overland Lim. 2 and Los Ang. Lim. 8 carry the vertical legends "See Special Notice on page 784" and "See Special Notice on page 785" across the local-stop rows; St'msburg Local ■28 carries "Via Beatrice and Stromsburg Branch."

Table 1. June, 1916.	Miles	San Fran. Lim. 10	Atl. Exp. 4	Colorado Spl. 12	Chicago Exp. 16	Omaha Exp. 6	Pacific Lim. 20	Ore.-Wash Lim. 18	Overland Lim. 2	Los Ang. Lim. 8	Denver Spl. 14	North Platte Local. ■26	Grand Isl. Local. ■24	St'msburg Local. ■28
Chicago (C. & N. W.) [ARRIVE	o	2 00	8 45	8 45	7 34	7 34	.....	11 00	9 30	11 30	2 00	7 34	6 45	7 34
Omaha » lve	491	1 20	7 30	7 30	6 00	6 00	.....	8 32	9 00	10 10	1 20	6 00	12 30	6 00
(C. M. & St. P.) lve...Chicago....arr	o	.....	9 05	9 05	8 10	8 10	9 15	.....	.....	.....	.....	8 10	8 10	8 10
arr....Omaha....lve	492	.....	7 10	7 10	6 05	6 05	7 50	.....	.....	.....	.....	6 05	6 05	6 05
(Central time.) lv.Council Bluffs.ar		1 35	7 20	7 35	4 35	5 25	8 15	8 40	9 20	10 25	1 35	5 05	10 55	12 55
arr....Omaha....lve		1 20	7 05	7 20	4 20	5 10	8 00	8 25	9 05	10 10	1 20	4 50	10 40	12 40
lve..+Omaha ♂..arr	o	12 55	6 50	7 00	4 00	5 00	7 35	8 15	8 45	9 55	1 05	4 45	10 30	12 30
...South Omaha...	4	.....	.....	.....	.....	.....	.....	.....	.....	.....	—	4 24	10 12	.....
....Gilmore.....	10	.....	.....	.....	.....	.....	.....	.....	.....	.....	—	4 08	9 57	.....
....Papillion.....	15	.....	.....	.....	.....	.....	.....	.....	.....	.....	—	3 55	9 47	.....
.....Millard.....	20	.....	.....	.....	.....	.....	.....	.....	.....	.....	—	3 43	9 35	.....
.....Elkhorn......	29	c m	—	h -	h -	c o	c -	—	See Spl. Notice p.784	x	—	3 28	9 19	11 47
...Waterloo......	31	c m	—	h -	h -	c o	c -	—		x	—	3 21	9 12	11 38
.....Valley..	35	c m	5 54	h -	h -	c o	c -	—		x	—	3 15	9 05	11 30
+....Fremont.....	46	11 51	5 34	5 50	2 50	3 52	6 28	7 01	7 41	8 44	11 50	2 55	8 48	Via Beatrice and Stromsburg Branch.
.....Ames........	53	c m	—	h -	h -	c o	c -	—		x	—	2 34	8 33	
+...North Bend....	61	c m	—	h -	h -	c o	c -	—		x	—	2 17	8 18	
+.....Rogers	68	c m	—	h -	h -	c o	c -	—		x	—	2 03	8 03	
+....Schuyler	76	c m	4 44	h -	2 00	c o	c -	6 14		x	—	1 48	7 50	
+....Richland	84	c m	—	h -	h -	c o	c -	—		x	—	1 33	7 35	
+....Columbus	91	10 48	4 20	4 45	1 36	2 49	5 21	5 53	6 44	7 40	10 48	1 20	7 20	
....Duncan......	99	c m	—	h -	h -	c o	c -	—		x	—	12 43	6 53	
....Silver Creek....	109	c m	—	h -	h -	c o	c -	5 25		x	—	12 25	6 36	
.....Havens	115	c m	—	h -	h -	c o	c -	—		x	—	12 13	6 26	
.....Clarks....	121	c m	—	h -	h -	c o	c -	5 09		x	—	12 04	6 17	
.....Thummel......	126	c m	—	h -	h -	c o	c -	—		x	—	11 53	6 07	
+...Central City..	132	9 54	3 15	h -	12 28	1 51	4 22	4 52		x	—	11 44	5 58	6 15
.....Paddock......	135	c m	—	h -	h -	c o	c -	—		x	—	11 37	—	
......Chapman	142	9 41	—	h -	h -	c o	c -	—		x	—	11 24	5 39	5 53
ar.+ Grand Island .lv.	154	9 25	2 45	3 15	11 50	1 20	3 50	4 20	5 25	6 10	9 20	11 05	*5 20	†5 30
lv. Grand Island ♂ ar.	154	9 20	2 40	3 10	11 45	11 00	3 45	4 15	5 20	6 05	9 15	10 50	A M	A M
.....Alda	161	c m	—	h -	h -	c o	c -	—		x	—	10 32	.....	.....
....Wood River.....	169	c m	2 10	h -	a h	c o	c -	3 53		x	—	10 18	.....	.....
.....Shelton	177	c m	1 55	h -	a h	c o	c -	3 39		x	—	10 03	.....	.....
......Gibbon......	183	c m	1 43	h -	a h	c o	c -	3 25		x	—	9 50	.....	.....
.....Buda	191	c m	—	h -	h -	c o	c -	—		x -	—	9 30	.....	.....
+....Kearney	196	*8 15	*1 19	*2 05	*10 38	*11 57	*2 41	*3 01	*4 20	*4 54	*8 10	*9 20	.....	.....
[ARRIVE		P M	A M	A M	A M	A M	P M	P M	P M	P M	P M	P M	A M	

● Trains Nos. 25, 27 and 23 leave U. P. Transfer (Council Bluffs) 7 35 a.m., 12 01 noon and 4 55 p.m., respectively. ■ Trains Nos. 24, 28 and 26 arrive U. P. Transfer 10 55 a.m., 12 55 noon and 5 05 p.m., respectively.

For explanation of signs, see following page. For Index of Stations, see pages 779-781. Continued on following page.

The June 1916 schedule Table 1 from the *Official Guide of the Railways* shows the extensive passenger service the Union Pacific Railroad had via its C&NW plus CM&St.P connections from Chicago, Illinois, to Omaha, Nebraska, and its own line from Omaha to Kearney, Nebraska.

790

UNION PACIFIC SYSTEM

New and Direct Route to Yellowstone National Park

UNION PACIFIC RAILROAD CO.

American Express Company.

Table 2—MAIN LINE OMAHA TO OGDEN—Continued.

June, 1916.

Westbound trains (read down): Kearney to Ogden.

Ms.	Station	11	25	5	19	18	15	3-21	7	17	1
		Noon	PM		AM	AM	PM	PM	PM	PM	Noon
196	**Kearney** [LEAVE	*1210	*3 55		*5 45	*4 51	*9 34	*1019	*4 19	*5 15	*1221
205	Odessa	—	4 13		—	—	—	—	—	—	—
211	Elm Creek	—	4 24		6 10	—	—	10 49	—	—	—
220	Overton	—	4 41		6 24	—	—	11 04	—	—	—
231	Lexington	12 57	5 02		6 45	5 38	10 30	11 26	5 10	4 08	1 08
239	Darr	—	5 20		—	—	—	11 48	—	—	—
245	Cozad	—	5 33		7 10	—	—	11 48	—	—	—
250	Willow Island	—	5 45		—	—	—	11 58	—	—	—
256	Gothenberg	—	5 58		7 32	—	—	12 11	—	—	—
268	Brady Island	—	6 23		7 57	—	—	12 30	—	—	—
277	Maxwell	—	6 44		8 16	—	—	12 48	—	—	—
291	ar.) **North** (C.T.)	2 25	7 15		8 45	—	10 50	12 10	6 40	5 45	2 40
291	lv.) **Platte** (M.T.)(ar.	1 35	PM	*4 02	7 50	6 15	11 20	12 30	5 45	4 50	1 45
304	Hershey	—	8 13		—	—	—	12 56	—	—	b —
308	O'Fallons	—	—		—	—	—	1 10	—	—	—
310	Sutherland	—	8 28		—	—	—	1 10	—	—	b —
322	Paxton	—	8 48		—	—	—	1 30	—	—	—
342	Ogallala	2 51	9 20		7 35	12 41	—	2 06	—	6 05	—
351	Brule	—	9 35		—	—	—	2 26	—	—	—
361	Big Springs	3 50	9 55		—	—	—	2 48	—	—	—
372	**Julesburg**	3 50	10 18		8 30	1 35	7 50	3 15	6 54	3 45	—
387	Chappell	PM	10 46		AM	AM	—	3 50	7 20	—	—
396	Lodge Pole	—	11 06		—	—	—	4 12	7 39	—	—
403	Sunol	—	—		—	—	—	4 26	—	—	—
414	**Sidney**	—	11 50		—	—	8 10	5 00	8 15	4 53	—
433	Potter	—	12 29		—	—	—	5 51	8 53	—	—
442	Dix	—	—		—	—	—	6 11	—	—	—
451	Kimball	—	—	1 02	—	—	—	6 37	9 28	—	—
463	Bushnell	—	—		—	—	—	7 06	—	—	—
473	Pine Bluffs	—	—	1 44	—	—	—	7 35	10 06	—	—
484	Egbert	—	—		—	—	—	8 09	—	—	—
490	Burns	—	—		—	—	—	8 33	—	—	—
496	Hillsdale	—	—		—	—	—	8 55	—	—	—
502	Durham	—	—		—	—	—	9 10	—	—	—
508	Archer	—	—		—	—	—	9 25	—	—	—
516	arr.+**Cheyenne**.lve	—	21	3 15	—	—	—	9 45	12 35	11 45	7 55
516	lve..**Cheyenne**.arr	—	PM *9 12	3 25	—	—	—	11 35	12 50	12 01	8 15
526	Borie	—	—		—	—	—	11 59	—	—	—
535	Granite Canon	—	—		—	—	—	12 21	—	—	—
543	Buford	—	—		—	—	—	12 39	—	—	—
547	Sherman	—	—		—	—	—	12 48	—	—	—
555	Hermosa	—	—		—	—	—	1 01	—	—	—
573	**Laramie**	—	5 40	11 01	5 25	—	—	1 55	2 50	2 10	10 20
592	Bosler	—	—		—	—	—	2 42	—	—	—
601	Lookout	—	—		—	—	—	3 07	—	—	—
612	**Rock River**	—	6 45		—	—	—	3 58	—	—	—
630	Medicine Bow	—	—		—	—	—	4 23	—	3 45	—
634	**Allen**	—	—		—	—	—	4 34	—	—	—
650	Hanna	—	7 51		—	—	—	5 18	—	4 23	—
669	Walcott	—	—		—	—	—	6 10	—	4 58	—
675	Fort Steele	—	—		—	—	—	6 25	—	5 08	—
690	**Rawlins**	—	8 05	1 53	8 50	—	—	7 05	5 55	5 40	1 30
719	Creston	—	—		—	—	—	8 01	—	—	—
731	Wamsutter	—	—	3 00	—	—	—	8 24	—	6 59	—
764	Bitter Creek	—	—		—	—	—	9 42	—	—	—
784	Point of Rocks	—	—		—	—	—	10 24	—	—	—
809	+.. Rock Springs	67	12 35	—	12 19	69	9	11 10	9 20	9 07	4 46
824	ar.+**Green River** lv.	AM 1 00	1 00	5 15	12 45	AM	AM	11 40	9 44	9 35	5 10
824	lve..**Green River** arr.	*9 40	1 20	5 25	12 50	*1 35	*1000	1 20	9 50	10 10	5 25
854	**Granger**	10 30	2 15	6 10	—	2 35	—	2 15	—	11 20	—
866	Church Buttes	10 47	2 32	AM	—	AM	—	2 32	—	AM	—
873	Hampton	10 57	2 44		—		—	2 44	—		—
883	**Carter**	11 13	2 58		—		—	2 58	—		—
893	Bridger	11 29	3 16				—	3 16	—		—
898	Leroy	11 36	3 24		—		—	3 24	—		—
905	Spring Valley	11 48	3 35		—		—	3 35	—		—
909	Aspen	11 55	3 42		—		—	3 42	—		—
911	Altamont	12 05	3 52		—		—	3 52	—		—
916	Knight	12 17	4 00		—		—	4 00	—		—
924	+... **Evanston**	‖1 10	4 20		4 05		1 00	4 20	1 08		8 10
935	Wahsatch	1 34	4 42		—		—	4 42	—		—
944	Castle Rock	1 52	5 04		—		—	5 04	—		—
960	**Echo**	2 25	5 34		5 20		—	5 34	—		—
969	Devil's Slide	2 50	5 51		—		—	5 51	—		—
976	Morgan	3 08	6 03		—		—	6 03	—		—
983	Peterson	3 28	6 17		—		—	6 17	—		—
993	Uintah	3 57	6 41		—		—	6 41	—		—
1000	+..... **Ogden** [ARRIVE	4 20	7 05		6 55		3 20	7 05	3 35		10 40
		PM	AM		AM		AM	PM	AM		AM

Eastbound trains (read down), same stations — Kearney to Ogden:

Ms.	Station	10	4-10	12	16	6	20	18	2	8	26	14
		PM	AM	AM	AM	AM	PM	PM	PM	PM	AM	PM
196	**Kearney** ARRIVE]	8 15	1 19	2 05	10 38	11 57	2 41	3 01	4 20	4 54	9 20	8 10
205	Odessa	—	—	—	—	—	—	—	—	—	8 56	—
211	Elm Creek	c —	12 50	h —	a h y	c o	c —	—	—	x —	8 42	—
220	Overton	c —	12 38	h —	h —	c o	c —	—	—	x —	8 24	—
231	Lexington	7 21	12 22	1 07	9 38	11 03	1 45	2 03	3 31	3 59	8 05	7 20
239	Darr	c —	—	h —	h —	c o	c —	—	—	x —	7 43	—
245	Cozad	c —	12 01	h —	9 15	c o	c —	1 48	—	x —	7 30	—
250	Willow Island	c —	11 52	h —	h —	c o	c —	—	—	x —	7 20	—
256	Gothenberg	c —	11 43	h —	8 56	c o	c —	1 33	—	x —	7 08	—
268	Brady Island	c —	11 24	h —	h —	c o	c —	—	—	x —	6 40	—
277	Maxwell	c —	11 11	h —	e h	c o	c —	—	—	x —	6 22	—
291	ar.) **North** (C.T.)	5 55	10 50	11 35	7 55	9 30	12 15	12 40	2 10	2 30	*6 00	5 50
291	lv.) **Platte** (M.T.)(ar.	4 50	9 40	10 25	6 45	8 10	11 10	11 35	1 05	1 25	AM	4 45
304	Hershey	c —	9 13	h —	h —	7 47	c —	—	—	x —	—	—
308	O'Fallons	c —	—	h —	h —	c —	c —	—	—	x —	—	—
310	Sutherland	c —	9 00	h —	h —	7 35	c —	—	—	x —	—	—
322	Paxton	c —	8 42	h —	h —	7 15	c —	—	—	x —	—	—
342	Ogallala	3 39	8 11	9 04	h —	6 48	c —	—	—	x —	—	—
351	Brule	c —	7 57	h —	h —	6 33	c —	—	—	x —	—	—
361	Big Springs	c —	7 38	h —	h —	6 16	c —	—	—	x —	—	—
372	**Julesburg**	2 56	7 21	*8 20	*4 30	5 57	—	9 34	11 16	11 29	—	*2 55
387	Chappell	c —	6 54	PM	AM	5 25	c —	—	—	x —	—	PM
396	Lodge Pole	c —	6 38	—	—	5 06	c —	—	—	x —	—	—
403	Sunol	c —	6 28	—	—	—	c —	—	—	x —	—	—
414	**Sidney**	1 53	6 10	—	—	4 35	8 10	8 30	10 15	10 25	—	—
433	Potter	c —	5 13	—	—	4 01	c —	—	—	x.—	—	—
442	Dix	—	4 56	—	—	—	—	—	—	—	—	—
451	Kimball	12 53	4 38	—	—	3 35	c —	—	—	x —	—	—
463	Bushnell	c —	4 15	—	—	c —	c —	—	—	x —	—	—
473	Pine Bluffs	12 22	3 55	—	—	3 04	—	—	—	—	—	—
484	Egbert	—	3 34	—	—	2 48	—	—	—	—	—	—
490	Burns	—	3 24	—	—	2 40	—	—	—	—	—	—
496	Hillsdale	—	3 14	—	—	2 31	—	—	—	—	—	—
502	Durham	—	3 04	—	—	—	—	—	—	—	—	—
508	Archer	—	2 55	—	—	—	—	—	—	—	—	—
516	arr.+**Cheyenne**.lve	11 20	2 35	—	22	2 00	5 35	5 55	7 45	7 50	—	—
516	lve..**Cheyenne**.arr	11 00	2 25	—	AM	1 45	5 20	5 40	7 35	7 30	—	—
526	Borie	—	1 59	—	9 30	—	—	—	—	—	—	—
535	Granite Canon	—	1 41	—	—	—	—	—	—	—	—	—
543	Buford	—	1 24	—	—	—	—	—	—	—	—	—
547	Sherman	—	1 16	—	—	—	—	—	—	—	—	—
555	Hermosa	—	1 01	—	—	—	—	—	—	—	—	—
573	**Laramie**	8 57	‖1222	—	7 52	11 45	3 25	3 40	5 45	5 35	—	—
592	Bosler	8 20	11 33	—	—	—	—	—	—	—	—	—
601	Lookout	—	11 17	—	—	—	—	—	—	—	—	—
612	**Rock River**	—	10 56	—	—	10 32	—	—	—	—	—	—
630	Medicine Bow	—	10 23	—	—	9 55	—	—	—	—	—	—
634	**Allen**	—	—	—	—	—	—	—	—	—	—	—
650	Hanna	—	9 46	—	—	9 15	—	—	—	—	—	—
669	Walcott	5 57	9 06	—	—	8 32	—	—	—	—	—	—
675	Fort Steele	—	8 54	—	—	8 20	—	—	—	—	—	—
690	**Rawlins**	5 20	‖8 30	—	4 33	‖7 50	11 40	11 55	2 41	2 02	—	—
719	Creston	—	7 20	—	—	—	—	—	—	—	—	—
731	Wamsutter	—	6 59	—	—	6 18	—	—	—	—	—	—
764	Bitter Creek	—	—	—	—	5 21	—	—	—	—	—	—
784	Point of Rocks	—	—	—	—	4 42	—	—	—	—	—	—
809	+.. Rock Springs	1 30	4 42	66	12 58	4 00	7 48	8 00	11 22	10 08	64	—
824	ar.+**Green River** lv.	1 00	4 15	AM	12 30	3 30	7 20	7 30	10 53	9 40	PM	—
824	lve..**Green River** arr.	12 50	12 50	3 58	12 15	3 13	7 10	7 20	10 48	9 35	2 50	—
854	**Granger**	11 59	11 59	*3 10	—	2 22	—	*6 25	—	—	*1 50	—
866	Church Buttes	11 39	11 39	AM	—	2 02	—	PM	—	—	PM	—
873	Hampton	11 29	11 29		—	1 51	—		—	—		—
883	**Carter**	11 14	11 14		—	1 35	—		—	—		—
893	Bridger	10 56	10 56		—	c —	—		—	—		—
898	Leroy	10 48	10 48		—	1 07	—		—	—		—
905	Spring Valley	10 35	10 35		—	12 54	—		—	—		—
909	Aspen	10 28	10 28		—	12 48	—		—	—		—
911	Altamont	10 18	10 18		—	12 38	—		—	—		—
916	Knight	10 08	10 08		—	c —	—		—	—		—
924	+... **Evanston**	9 50	9 50		9 15	‖12 01	4 05		7 58	6 45		—
935	Wahsatch	9 20	9 20		—	11 20	—		—	—		—
944	Castle Rock	8 56	8 56		—	10 57	—		—	—		—
960	**Echo**	8 23	8 23		—	10 23	—		—	—		—
969	Devil's Slide	8 02	8 02		—	10 00	—		—	—		—
976	Morgan	7 44	7 44		—	c —	—		—	—		—
983	Peterson	7 26	7 26		—	9 25	—		—	—		—
993	Uintah	7 03	7 03		—	8 58	—		—	—		—
1000	+..... **Ogden** [LEAVE	*6 45	*6 45		*6 35	*8 40	*1 20		*5 10	*3 40		—
		PM	PM		PM	AM	PM		PM	PM		—

Connecting lines from Ogden (westbound, left trains):

(O. S. L. R. R.)

Station	11	25	19	15	3-21	7	1
lve.. **Ogden** ..arr.	*4 50	*7 30	*7 30	*4 00	7 30	*4 00	*1055
arr. **Salt Lake City**..lve	5 55	8 20	8 30	5 00	8 30	5 00	11 55
arr.**Yellowstone**.lve.	PM	AM	PM	AM	AM		AM

(So. Pac. Co.)

Station	11	25	19	15	3-21	1
lve... **Ogden** ..arr.	AM	6 30	6 30	6 30	3 40	9 55
arr. **Sacramento**.lve.	5 50	5 50	5 50	3 50		6 40
San Francisco	9 30	9 30	9 30	7 50		10 10
arr. **Los Angeles**.lve.	2 30	2 30	2 30	4 50		2 30

Connecting lines from Ogden (eastbound, right trains):

(O. S. L. R. R.)

Station	10	4-10	16	6	20	2	8
lve.. **Ogden** ..arr.	6 20	6 20	6 20	8 20	1 05	4 30	3 50
arr. **Salt Lake City**..lve	*5 15	*5 15	*5 15	*7 20	‡1205	*3 30	*2 30
arr.**Yellowstone**.lve.	PM	PM	PM	‡AM	Noon	PM	PM

(So. Pac. Co.)

Station	10	4-10	16	6	20	2
lve... **Ogden** ..arr.	PM	PM	PM	AM	PM	PM
arr. **Sacramento**.lve.	5 20	5 20	5 20	*1055	1 45	*7 15
San Francisco	*1 40	*1 40	*1 40	*7 00	1020	*4 00
arr. **Los Angeles**.lve.				*8 00	9 00	*1 25

Via Salt Lake Route.

Note (col. 18/15 of lower section, vertical): ‡ Service to Yellowstone National Park only during season, June 15th to September 16th.

The June 1916 schedule Table 2 from the *Official Guide of the Railways* shows Union Pacific Railroad passenger service from Kearney, Nebraska, to Ogden, Utah, with Southern Pacific Company service from Ogden to San Francisco and Los Angeles.

CHICAGO — SAN FRANCISCO—via Omaha

WESTBOUND
Read Down

EASTBOUND
Read Up

Domeliner City of San Francisco 103-SP 101 ● Example		Table **B** Condensed Schedules ■ Tri-Weekly		Domeliner City of San Francisco SP 102-UP 104 ● Example	
		C. M. St. P. & P.			
	6.00 SUN	Lv **Chicago** (C.S.T.)	Ar	12.40 WED	
	8.33 "	" Savanna	"	9.55 "	
	10.06 "	" Marion (Cedar Rapids)	"	8.15 "	
	12.12 MON	" Perry	Ar	5.58 "	
	2.50 MON	Ar **Omaha**	Lv	3.50 WED	
		Union Pacific			
	3.15 MON	Lv **Omaha**	Ar	3.15 WED	
	3.55 "	" Fremont	Lv	2.14 "	
	4.33 "	" Columbus	"	1.23 "	
	5.35 "	" Grand Island	"	12.25 WED	
	6.17 "	" Kearney	"	11.27 TUE	
	7.50 "	Ar North Platte (C.S.T.)	Lv	9.40 "	
	◄ 7.05 "	Lv North Platte (M.S.T.)	Ar	◄ 8.25 "	
See Note	8.50 "	" Sidney	"	See Note	6.30 "
	10.25 "	Ar **Cheyenne**	Lv	4.55 "	
	11.05 "	Lv **Cheyenne**	Ar	4.25 "	
	12.28 "	" Laramie	Lv	3.05 "	
	2.17 "	" Rawlins	"	1.21 "	
	4.07 "	" Rock Springs	"	11.25 "	
	4.40 "	Ar Green River	Lv	11.05 "	
	5.05 "	Lv Green River	Ar	10.45 "	
	6.59 "	" Evanston	Lv	9.00 "	
	8.50 MON	Ar **Ogden** (M.S.T.)	Lv	7.30 TUE	
		Southern Pacific Ø			
	10.30 MON	Lv **Ogden** (M.S.T.)	Ar	7.00 TUE	
	7.30 TUE	" Reno (P.S.T.)	Lv	8.02 MON	
	8.25 "	" Truckee	"	7.00 "	
	12.30 "	Ar Sacramento	Lv	3.20 "	
	12.45 "	Lv Sacramento	Ar	3.10 "	
	2.57 "	Ar Berkeley	Lv	1.10 "	
	3.15 "	" Oakland (16th St.)	"	1.00 "	
	3.45 TUE	Ar **San Francisco** (P.S.T.)	Lv	12.30 MON	

NO. 103-SP 101; SP 102-UP 101 — *Domeliner* **CITY OF SAN FRANCISCO — TRI-WEEKLY — See Note ■**

Trains run via C. M. St. P. & P. Chicago—Omaha; U. P. Omaha—Ogden; S. P. Ogden—San Francisco.

Coach Seat Reservation Charge — See Page 28.

Dome Lounge Car ⊗ ..... Chicago—Ogden.
Streamlined Sleeping Car ..Chicago—San Francisco—Double Bedrooms, Roomettes
Reclining Seat—
  Leg Rest Coach .... Chicago—San Francisco—all seats reserved.
        Cheyenne—San Francisco (No. 9-10 — From Kansas City—leg rest seats, all reserved).
Cafe Lounge Car .... Omaha—Ogden; Ogden—San Francisco—moderately priced meals and lounge for coach passengers.
Dome Dining Car..... Chicago—Ogden—club and a la carte service.
Dining Car .... Ogden—San Francisco—club and a la carte service.

Passengers use Motor Bus between trainside at Oakland (16th Street) and San Francisco (3rd and Townsend Station) via the Bay Bridge, affording a panoramic view of the San Francisco Bay area.

■ Operates from Chicago Sunday, Wednesday & Friday; from San Francisco Monday, Thursday & Saturday.

⊗ These lounge cars are for exclusive use of sleeping car passengers. The City of San Francisco has a lounge car for coach passengers.

Ø Subject to Southern Pacific special "City of San Francisco" charge.

● Limited handling of checked baggage on this train; consult agent.

ⓔ Conditional stop; see Table 1.

(M.S.T.) Mountain standard time.

(C.S.T.) Central standard time.

(P.S.T.) Pacific standard time.

Time from 12:01 midnight to 12:00 noon shown in light face type.

Time from 12.01 noon to 12.00 midnight shown in heavy face type.

CHICAGO—OMAHA—DENVER

WESTBOUND
Read Down

EASTBOUND
Read Up

Advance Coach Seat Reservations Required	City of Denver 103-111 Example	Table **C** Condensed Schedules All Trains Daily		City of Denver 112-104 Example	Advance Coach Seat Reservations Required
		C. M. St. P. & P.			
	6.00 SUN	Lv **Chicago** (C.S.T.)	Ar	12.40 MON	
	2.50 MON	Ar **Omaha**	Lv	3.50 "	
		Union Pacific			
	3.15 MON	Lv **Omaha** (C.S.T.)	Ar	3.15 MON	
	3.55 "	" Fremont	Lv	2.14 "	
	4.53 "	" Columbus	"	1.23 "	
	5.35 "	" Grand Island	"	12.25 "	
	6.17 "	" Kearney	◄	11.27 SUN	
	◄ 7.50 "	Ar **North Platte** (C.S.T.)	Lv	9.40 "	
See Note	7.10 "	Lv **North Platte** (M.S.T.)	Ar	8.00 "	See Note
	f8.00 "	" Ogallala	Lv	f7.10 "	
	8.31 "	" Julesburg	"	6.40 "	
	9.29 "	ⓔ Sterling	"	5.45 "	
	ⓔ	" Fort Morgan			
	10.58 "	" La Salle	"	4.14 "	
	11.59 MON	Ar **Denver** (M.S.T.)	Lv	3.15 SUN	

NO. 103-111; 112-104— CITY OF DENVER—DAILY

Trains run via C. M. St. P. & P. Chicago—Omaha; U. P. Omaha—Denver

Coach Seat Reservation Charge—See Page 28.

Reclining Seat—
  Leg Rest Coaches ..... Chicago—Denver (all seats reserved).
        Omaha—Denver (all seats reserved).
Cafe-Lounge Car .... North Platte—Denver Meal service, and beverages.
Dining Car .... Chicago—North Platte
Dome Lounge Car .... Chicago—North Platte

▲ Special Coach Seat Reservation Charge—See Page 28.

ⓔ Stops to let off or take paying passengers to or from points where these trains are regularly scheduled to stop.

(f) Stops only on signal.

(C.S.T.) Central Standard time.   (M.S.T.) Mountain Standard time.

Time from 12.01 midnight to 12.00 noon shown in light face type.

Time from 12.01 noon to 12.00 midnight shown in heavy face type.

The April 26, 1970 Union Pacific Railroad Table B shows the *City of San Francisco* tri-weekly Sunday, Wednesday, and Friday schedule from Chicago via Omaha, Nebraska; North Platte, Nebraska; and Ogden, Utah, to San Francisco and the *City of San Francisco* tri-weekly schedule Monday, Thursday, and Saturday schedule from San Francisco to Chicago. Table C shows the *City of Denver* daily service between Chicago via Omaha, Nebraska, and North Platte, Nebraska, to Denver, Colorado. (*Beth Anne Keates Collection*)

A Southern Pacific Company steam locomotive is heading a passenger train on the railroad's Coast Line connecting San Francisco with Los Angeles via San Jose, Santa Cruz, and San Luis Obispo in this scenic postcard scene around the 1920s. According to the *June 1916 Official Guide of the Railways*, there were six passenger trains daily in each direction on the Southern Pacific's Coast Line. (*Kenneth C. Springirth collection*)

On August 6, 1967, Virginia Springirth, wife of co-author Kenneth C. Springirth, is at the Green River, Wyoming, Union Pacific Railroad passenger station. This was their first long-distance railroad passenger trip to San Francisco to ride and photograph streetcars. (*Kenneth C. Springirth photograph*)

Standing on the Green River, Sweetwater County, Wyoming, platform of the Union Pacific Railroad passenger station on August 6, 1967 is Kenneth C. Springirth, co-author of this book, alongside Milwaukee Road car No. 651 which was part of the *City of San Francisco* Union Pacific Railroad passenger train. This was an operational stop for that train that allowed some quick photography. The Union Pacific reached Green River on October 1, 1868 bringing the outside world to that area. (*Virginia M. Springirth photograph*)

Union Pacific Railroad 2,250-horsepower EMD type E8A passenger train locomotives Nos. 927 (built in 1950 and retired in 1972) and 935 (built in 1953 and retired in 1969) are waiting for their next assignment at Green River, Wyoming, on August 6, 1967. There were a total of eighteen E8A locomotives (Nos. 925–942) by 1953. Eventually there were forty-six E8 and sixty-nine E9 locomotives that became the UP's most famous passenger service motive power. (*Kenneth C. Springirth photograph*)

On August 6, 1967, the westbound Union Pacific Railroad train *City of San Francisco* is passing through Weber Canyon which is near Ogden, Utah. Named for fur trapper John Henry Weber, the first road through the canyon was completed in 1855. The Union Pacific Railroad built the transcontinental railroad through Weber Canyon. (*Kenneth C. Springirth photograph*)

On April 30, 1971, the Chicago, Milwaukee, St. Paul & Pacific Railroad train No. 103, the combined *City of Los Angeles*, *City of San Francisco*, *City of Portland*, and *City of Kansas* departs Chicago for its last run on April 30, 1971 headed by Union Pacific Railroad 2,400-horsepower diesel passenger train locomotive No. 912 (EMD type E9A built in December 1963 and retired in 1972). (*Photographer John A. Kirchner Used with permission from Audio-Visual Designs [www.audiovisualdesigns.com]*)

9

Union Pacific Locomotives on Display

ody Park and Railroad Museum 1400 N. Jeffers Street, North Platte, Nebraska, has Union Pacific Railroad Challenger No. 3977, with a 4-6-6-4 wheel arrangement built by American Locomotive Company (Alco) in June 1943, retired in 1961, and placed in Cody Park in October 1968 on static display. There were 105 Challengers built with their design influencing the Big Boy design plus influenced the design of the last three orders of Challengers. While they operated mainly in freight service, a few were assigned to passenger service. In addition, Cody Park has 6,600-horsepower No. 6922 locomotive EMD type DDA40X (with the X meaning experimental) built in December 1969. Locomotive No. 6900 was delivered in April 1969 followed by 6901–6924 by December1969. Over the next two years, locomotives Nos. 6925–6946 were delivered completing the forty-seven-unit order. No. 6922 was donated to Cody Park in 1985.

The North Carolina Transportation Museum 411 S. Salisbury Avenue, Spencer, North Carolina, site of the Southern Railway's former Spencer steam locomotives' repair shops, hosted in 2014 Union Pacific diesel locomotive No. 949 EMD type E9 that was built in May 1955.

The Illinois Railway Museum 7000 Olson Road in Union, Illinois, has Union Pacific Railroad No. 18 General Electric 8,500-horsepower type 8500 GTEL (gas turbine electric locomotive) built in August 1960 and No. 1848 General Electric type 4,000-horsepower type B40-8 built in August 1988 used on the Cotton Belt as No. 8049 during 1988 to 1999, became Union Pacific No. 5657 during 1999 to 2002, renumbered 1848 during 2002–2014, and has been at the Illinois Railway Museum since 2014.

Steamtown National Historic Site 350 Cliff Street, Scranton, Pennsylvania, has Union Pacific Railroad Big Boy No. 4012.

The National Railway Museum 2285 South Broadway, Green Bay, Wisconsin has Union Pacific Railroad Union Pacific Big Boy locomotive No. 4017 that is housed in a climate-controlled facility.

On display at the 100-acre Cody Park in North Platte, Nebraska, in August 2019 is retired UP challenger type steam locomotive No. 3977. The 121.83-foot-long locomotive weighed 627,900 pounds, and tender weighed 446,000 pounds. Tender capacity was 28 tons of coal or 5,945 gallons of oil, and 25,000 gallons of water. This locomotive had a maximum speed of 70 miles per hour. (*Beth Anne Keates photograph*)

In August 2019, Union Pacific Railroad 6,600-horsepower diesel electric locomotive No. 6922 (EMD type DDA40X with X meaning experimental) is on display at Cody Park in North Platte, Nebraska. There were forty-seven of these 98.415-foot-long locomotives (Nos. 6900–6946) with the first unit No. 6900 (nicknamed Centennial) arriving in Salt Lake City, Utah, on May 10, 1969 to commemorate the centennial anniversary of completion of the First Transcontinental Railroad. Although their performance was excellent, they were costly to maintain and were all retired by 1986. (*Beth Anne Keates photograph*)

Union Pacific Railroad passenger hauling diesel 2,400-horsepower locomotive No. 949 (EMD type E9 built in May 1955) weighed 167.8 tons, had a length of 70.25 feet over pulling faces, and a top speed of 98 miles per hour according to Union Pacific data. This locomotive was on display in 2014 at the North Carolina Transportation Museum in Spencer, North Carolina. Locomotives Nos. 949, 951, and 963B were reacquired by the Union Pacific to handle bigger trains, and are used in special excursion service. (*Bob Elder photograph*)

The Illinois Railway Museum on September 5, 2021 at Union, Illinois, is the location of Union Pacific Railroad 8,500-horsepower No. 18 (GE type 8500 GTEL [gas turbine electric locomotive] built in 1960). This A unit had the control cab and auxiliary diesel generator, and the B unit had the turbine and main generators to provide electricity to the traction motors in both the A and B units. The locomotive weighed 849,248 pounds. (*Brian A. Keates photograph*)

On September 5, 2021, the Illinois Railway Museum at Union, Illinois, has former Union Pacific Railroad four-axle 4,000-horsepower diesel electric locomotive No. 1848 (GE type Dash 8-40B built in August 1988) pulling a caboose train. From 1988 to 1999, this locomotive (designed as a road switcher for general freight service) was used on the St. Louis Southwestern Railroad as No. 8049. From 1999 to 2002, it was Union Pacific No. 5657. It was renumbered Union Pacific No. 1848 in 2000 and in July 2014 was donated by the Union Pacific Railroad to the Illinois Railway Museum. (*Brian A. Keates photograph*)

The Steamtown National Historic Site at Scranton, Pennsylvania, on a snowy November 28, 2021 is the location of Union Pacific Railroad Big Boy No. 4012. This locomotive had powered Union Pacific Railroad freight trains for twenty-one years between Cheyenne, Wyoming, and Ogden, Utah. The locomotive was donated to Steamtown founded by Francis Nelson Blount and was on display at Bellows Falls, Vermont from 1962 to 1984 after which Steamtown was moved to Scranton, Pennsylvania. Following a cosmetic restoration that was completed on May 5, 2021, No. 4012 was returned for static display. (*Brian A. Keates photograph*)

On October 6, 1958, Union Pacific Big Boy No. 4017 makes a coaling stop at Harriman, Wyoming. This locomotive was retired in May 1961 and is on display at the National Railroad Museum at Green Bay, Wisconsin. (*Photographer Robert F. Collins Used with permission from Audio-Visual Designs [www.audiovisualdesigns.com]*)